UK

PHILIP JODIDIO

ARCHITECTURE IN THE UNITED KINGDOM

#2

#3/13

#5

#9/15

#14

#10

#1/1

#9/15

#7/12

#2

LONDON

INTRODUCTION

ADVENTURES IN THE SHIRE

The cover of a recent Spanish magazine featuring contemporary British architecture resembled nothing so much as an advertisement for *The War of the Worlds*. Hulking over the austere white and gray forms of David Chipperfield's London studio for Antony Gormley, the improbable shapes of Future Systems' Selfridges store in Birmingham and Will Alsop's College of Art and Design in Toronto appeared to be doing gruesome battle over some decidedly insular territory. The Spanish photomontage gives no clue as to which style would be the victor, but it does hint at the remarkable variety seen in the contemporary architecture of the United Kingdom. Although some prestigious and creative English-based designers, ranging from Lord Norman Foster to Zaha Hadid and Foreign Office Architects (FOA), do their most important work outside the UK, a brief overview of recent building in the country shows solutions varying from minimalist rigor to pop art excess. But then few other countries manage to simultaneously nurture centuries-old traditions while spawning musical groups like the Sex Pistols. Or perhaps stark contrast and deeply divided aesthetics are just a sign of the times. The English fashion designer John Galliano has run roughshod over the staid lines of Dior, somehow giving new luster to a worn-out brand. Inspiration for young architects, too? And if English design triumphs abroad, just how insular can it really be? In the image of London itself, contemporary architecture in the UK is something of a cosmopolitan melting pot. Architects featured in this book and based mostly in the capital were born in Baghdad, Dar-Es-Salaam, Shiraz, Madrid, Zlin (Czech Republic), or Poole, Dorset. The point of this volume is not to give an exhaustive evaluation of architecture in the UK, but to select a number of very recent buildings that, taken together, are something of a barometer of the situation in 2005.

ONCE UPON A TIME...

No matter how large the infusion of foreign creativity in the UK's architectural gene pool, it remains that what happens today evolved from a tradition. Inventiveness and occasional eccentricity are just part of what the place is about, as a tour of London's Victoria & Albert Museum's English galleries clearly shows. British Architecture of today must be seen against the background of the work of figures such as Alison and Peter Smithson, James Stirling, Cedric Price or Archigram. It may not be surprising that one of the most exotic recent English creations outside the UK was the work of Peter Cook, a former member of Archigram. His "friendly alien," a bulbous creature set down in the traditionally minded heart of Graz, Austria, is actually the city's new Kunsthaus (designed with Colin Fournier). Other architects have actively explored the idea of the "blob" in architecture, but few would have dared to juxtapose such an apparently amorphous musing in the middle of so much old stone and red tile. James Stirling, with buildings such as his Leicester Engineering Building (1959–63) or later work like the Clore Gallery at Tate Britain (Millbank), has done much to set the tone for English creativity in more recent years. Like the unexpected purple door in a London street, Stirling's post-Modern Clore Gallery shows a very British sense of color, erupting where it is least expected, reminding visitors that, beneath the surface, all may not be as calm as it seems. It was at Yale, where Stirling was teaching at the time, that Norman Foster and Richard Rogers met, shortly thereafter creating their partnership Team 4. Though much of Modernism carried with it the inspiration of the machine, it was in England that the most fruitful experimentation with mechanical shapes flourished, coming to carry the name of "High Tech" in the hands of Rogers, Foster and others. The astonishing colors and shapes of the Centre Georges Pompidou in Paris (Piano & Rogers, 1977) could hardly bear more obvious marks of their paternity. Like a machine turned inside-out with its tubes and ladders hanging out for all to see, or an unlikely aircraft carrier moored in the ancient Beaubourg district of Paris, the Centre Pompidou was an Archigram drawing come to life. "We were young and we wanted to be very much in their faces," confides a somewhat more sage Renzo Piano today. Contextualism has not always been a quality of contemporary architecture in the UK, where rupture and surprise have often been seen as the only possible response to immobility or heaviness. Naturally some did not agree with this analysis. Denys Lasdun for one created the National Theatre in London and much of the weighty architecture of the University of East Anglia, Norwich (beginning in 1962). The UK is also the land of Brutalism, where gray concrete sometimes rhymes sadly with gray skies.

THE LORDS OF TECH

Because they are Lords in the very English noble sense of the word, but more because their architecture has marked the contemporary landscape as much as that of any builder alive, Richard Rogers and Norman Foster deserve special mention in any overview of the UK. Modern London is shaped by Rogers' Lloyd's of London Headquarters (1978–86), as much as by Foster's more recent Swiss Re Headquarters (featured here, 1997–2004). Winner of the 1985 RIBA Gold Medal and the 2000 Praemium Imperiale, currently working on Terminal 5 at London's Heathrow Airport (1989–2008) and the National Assembly of Wales building in Cardiff, Rogers remains an international reference, perhaps more tied to his High-Tech past than his former partner. Winner of the Royal Gold Medal for Architecture (1983) and the American Institute of Architects Gold Medal (1994), Lord Norman Foster has brought his methodical and innovative approach to materials and designs to such diverse projects as the Airport at Chek Lap Kok, Hong Kong (1995–98); the new German Parliament (Reichstag, Berlin, 1995–99); or the British Museum Redevelopment (London, 1997–2000). The Millennium Bridge (1996–2002) crossing the Thames between St Paul's Cathedral and Tate Modern is his design as is the nearby Greater London Authority (1998–2002). Fascinated not only by materials but by engineering, Foster also designed the enormous Millau Viaduct in France (1993–2005). Defining his own approach to design and materials, Foster has said, "I care intensely about the appearance, but I don't think that the appearance is a matter of cosmetics. I don't think that it has too much to do with what I did or did not have for breakfast this morning. It doesn't mean to say that because it is massively informed by nature that it is automatically going to be beautiful. On the main flight path into Heathrow, we can gaze up and see some of the ugliest brutes flying overhead. Some are absolutely stunning. That has to do with the way the designers have interpreted those forces and those pressures. That is where it starts. It doesn't start with someone saying, what kind of aircraft shall we have today. Shall we have a sort of Sopwith Camel?"

Only slightly younger than Foster and Rogers, Nicholas Grimshaw is another innovative English architect who is fascinated by technology in his designs. His most visible project may be the International Terminal of Waterloo Station (London, 1988–93) that is seen by every incoming Eurostar passenger. "Good detailing comes first and foremost, then making buildings understandable spatially and organizationally," says Grimshaw, who built this 400-meter-long addition to London's Waterloo Station. Color is exceptionally part of the design in the form of the bright blue roof trusses, in a building that looks back to the heritage of such engineers or architects as Joseph Paxton, Gustave Eiffel, Pierre Chareau, and Jean Prouvé. A curved form imposed by the turning radius of the trains and the nature of the site led Grimshaw to use a "loose fit" of overlapping glass panes that admit ample light to the track areas. "Fitting in," says Grimshaw, "has to do with things like scale and height, light and shade, the feeling that a building has at ground level, at people level... It's not to do with just matching the building next door." His Eden Project (St Austell, Cornwall, 1998–2005) featured here is a remarkable cross between high-tech and ecological assertiveness that blends to create an environment that is indeed well named.

Concern for ecology is a strong point in the practice of another architect of the generation of Rogers and Foster, Michael Hopkins. Having worked with Foster and his wife Wendy between 1968 and 1976, Hopkins won the RIBA Gold Medal in 1994 together with his own wife. As Hopkins states, "Since we started in 1976 we have pioneered a series of strategies including fabric roofs, lightweight structures, energy efficient design, weaving new structures into existing ones, and recycling brown land." Michael Hopkins, like his colleagues born in the 1930s, has brought architecture in the UK to new heights, redefining modern goals in a systematic and innovative way, moving progressively more and more toward "green" designs that are not at all incompatible with the original technical orientation of those concerned.

KNIGHTS OF DRY CHIC

Though it is often artificial to group architects together under an aesthetic banner, it seems clear that a new generation of architects born after the War have taken new directions that are presently reshaping the face of what is built in the UK and abroad. The best known of these may be David Chipperfield, who worked in the offices of Norman Foster and Richard Rogers, before establishing his own firm in 1984. Though he is engaged in high-profile, long-term projects like the Neues Museum (Berlin, 2000–09) or the San Michele Cemetery (Venice, Italy, 1998–2013), Chipperfield's work is well exemplified by the rigor of the Antony Gormley Studio (London, 2001–03) featured here. Although Chipperfield has designed a number of fashion boutiques, there is more than a chic minimalism in his work. In the case of the Gormley Studio, there is a sublimated reference to industrial architecture and a functionality that make it clear that this is very serious architecture. A composition in gray and white, the architecture steps back to allow the creativity of the sculptor Antony Gormley to express itself. This is not a statement of modesty as much as it is a real understanding of what modern architecture is all about.

Though it may be that they are intentionally less given to minimalist perfection than Chipperfield, architects David Adjaye and Caruso St John subscribe to a pared down austerity that plays on subtlety and intelligence more than heavy-handed extravagance. Adjaye, born in 1966, who worked in the office of Chipper-

field in the early 1990s, is one of the rising stars of architecture in the UK, partly because he has worked for famous clients, but also because he has broken with convention. Delving into his recent work, including the Idea Store featured here, in the gap between the street and an intellectual approach to architecture, he says, "I'm trying to speak a language of mutual understanding between both worlds." With works such as their radical refurbishment of a former municipal garage near Kings Cross Station for the Gagosian Gallery, Caruso St John Architects have shown a capacity for practicality even as they display a rigorous will to do away with the superficial.

FUN ON THE FRINGE

As wild as Peter Cook's "Friendly Alien" in Graz may be, it pales in comparison to Will Alsop's College of Art and Design in Toronto. Apparently inspired by El Lissitzky's work, it looks more like a Memphis dining room table on steroids. A "hovering box" containing classrooms set on twelve 29-meter stilts, the design was accepted by the city of Toronto despite being completely outside local architectural norms. Born in 1947, Will Alsop worked in the office of Cedric Price (1973–77) and has maintained an active interest in art, as is clearly expressed in the 25-ton "structural scribble" that rises from the top of his Ben Pimlott Building (St James, New Cross, London, 2003–05) at Goldsmiths College featured here. The cancellation of some of Alsop's projects recently led to a reorganization of his office, but he remains convinced that architecture in the UK does not take enough risks and he has openly stated: "We had already decided that our future lies in North America, the Far East and Moscow, because there's not much happening in our traditional hunting grounds in Europe ..."

Some architects of course restrict their real flights of fancy to less public work. This may be the case of Laurie Chetwood, whose Butterfly House is a thoroughly unexpected "experiment in architectural sculpture." Inspired by the proliferation of butterflies near a house he bought, he proceeded to remodel it entirely based on the shapes and colors of the insects. Though it is founded on very sound principles, the Butterfly stands apart, even when the great variety of contemporary styles being practiced in the UK is taken into account. This is a rare case of a serious, professional architect, whose office won a "Practice of the Year" award in 2000, letting his imagination run free.

Chetwood's Butterfly House clearly has an ecological orientation, if only because of the garden "conceived as a perfect butterfly habitat." Many others in the UK have explored sustainability and other "green" issues in a varity of ways. Edward Cullinan, born in London in 1931, actually worked under Denys Lasdun (1958–65), and specifically on the student housing at the University of East Anglia, a surprising fact given that his much more recent Downland Gridshell (Singleton, West Sussex, 2000–02) shows a genuine concern for ecology with such features as untreated timber floors, ample natural light and the use of the thermal mass in the soil to control temperature. Above all, Cullinan represents a different direction that contemporary architecture can take, without heeding any dominant trend. He is an inventive and interesting figure.

MASTERS OF MAKEOVER

Bringing a truly modern feeling and functionality to old buildings, be they residential or industrial, is obviously a need in contemporary architecture that will have a long life. Although neither is truly specialized in makeovers, both Eva Jiricna and Dominic Williams of Ellis Williams have been particularly successful in different ways at breathing new life into existing structures. Jiricna certainly has her credentials as a modern designer, having been responsible for the interior design of the Lloyd's Headquarters. She has created boutiques for Hugo Boss, Joseph, and Joan & David, often creating spectacular sculptural staircases. Williams took on the dirtier job of making an old industrial flourmill into a museum (Baltic Centre for Contemporary Arts, Newcastle, UK, 1999–2002). Born in 1965, Dominic Williams worked at Skidmore, Owings and Merrill (1991–94) before joining the Ellis Williams Partnership in 1994. He represents a younger generation who are sensitive to issues ranging from the relationship of art to architecture, to ecological concerns.

WOMEN ON TOP

Although architecture in the UK has long been a male-dominated bastion, two women featured in this publication are clearly leading international figures. Both, perhaps coincidentally, were born in the Middle East. Zaha Hadid hardly needs to be introduced, particularly after her 2004 Pritzker Prize. Aside from being the first woman to win this prestigious prize, she is one of three architects based in the UK to have won this prize (after James Stirling in 1981, and Norman Foster in 1999), which places her in good company indeed. Following a pattern pioneered by such architects as her former partner in OMA, Rem Koolhaas, she established a considerable reputation with theoretical or more precisely visually oriented proposals. Her style of drawing was noted and figured prominently in such important exhibitions as the Deconstructivist Architecture show at New York's MoMA. Zaha Hadid has made a smooth transition from unbuilt proposals to major buildings, although her most significant work, such as the recent Rosenthal Centre for Contemporary Art (Cincinnati, Ohio, 1999–2003), and the Central Building of the BMW Assembly Plant in Leipzig (2005), remains outside the UK.

Farshid Moussavi of Foreign Office Architects (FOA) is hardly as well known as Zaha Hadid, but with her partner Alejandro Zaera Polo, she too is redefining the forms and approaches of contemporary architecture. She worked for the Renzo Piano Building Workshop in Genoa in 1988 and for the Office for Metropolitan Architecture in Rotterdam (Rem Koolhaas, 1991–93), while establishing FOA in 1992. The pair's widely published Yokohama International Port Terminal (Yokohama, Japan, 2000–02) broke new ground, almost literally. As they have written, "Rather than developing the building as an object or figure on the pier, the project is produced as an extension of the urban ground, constructed as a systematic transformation of the lines of the circulation diagram into a folded and bifurcated surface—the folded ground distributes the loads through the surfaces themselves, moving them diagonally to the ground."

Born in Shiraz, Iran, Moussavi, like Hadid, is a representative of a different breed of architect, a figure less and less attached to a specifically local identity. Few would characterize Zaha Hadid as an Iraqi architect, but not many would find her work specifically English either. This is not to say that globetrotters like Foster or Hadid propose catchall "globalized" solutions to the problems of contemporary architecture. Indeed, they are particularly sensitive to the needs of a given site, no matter what country it is in. Obviously, not every architect today has the background and the wherewithal to sustain a truly international career, nor even the desire for that matter. Computer-assisted design and communications do facilitate the task of figures like Hadid and Moussavi, and their presence in London transforms the definitions previously applied to the architectural profession. Fortunately there will always be architects who prefer to assume a purely local identity, but London today is the home base to some of the most important international architects, a situation that is not likely to change for the worse anytime soon.

Philip Jodidio

EINLEITUNG

ABENTEUER AUF DER INSEL

Das Titelblatt einer unlängst erschienenen spanischen Zeitschrift, die sich mit zeitgenössischer britischer Architektur beschäftigt, erinnert stark an eine Werbung für den *Krieg der Welten*: Über den weißen und grauen Formen von David Chipperfields Londoner Atelier von Antony Gormley dräuend, scheinen die bizarren Silhouetten des von Future Systems erbauten Selfridges Store in Birmingham und des College of Art and Design in Toronto von Will Alsop schauerliche Kämpfe um ein fraglos insulares Gebiet auszutragen. Der spanischen Fotomontage ist kein Hinweis zu entnehmen, welcher Stil den Sieg davontragen wird, aber sie spielt an auf die bemerkenswert vielfältigen Varianten der zeitgenössischen Architektur Großbritanniens. Obwohl einige in England ansässige renommierte, kreative Architekten von Lord Norman Foster bis zu Zaha Hadid oder Foreign Office Architects (FOA), die Mehrzahl ihrer wichtigen Bauten außerhalb Großbritanniens realisieren, zeigt ein kurzer Überblick über neuere Bauten in England Lösungen, die von minimalistischer Strenge bis zu Exzessen à la Pop-Art reichen. Freilich gelingt es wenigen anderen Ländern, gleichzeitig jahrhundertealte Traditionen zu pflegen und Musikgruppen wie die Sex Pistols hervorzubringen. Vielleicht sind krasse Gegensätze und zutiefst gespaltene ästhetische Vorstellungen nur ein Zeichen der Zeit. Der englische Modedesigner John Galliano ging rücksichtslos über die seriösen Formen von Dior hinweg und verhalf dabei einem angestaubten Markennamen zu neuem Glanz. Auch eine Anregung für junge Architekten? Und wenn englisches Design im Ausland Triumphe feiert, wie insular kann es dann wirklich sein? Ebenso wie London selbst gleicht die zeitgenössische Architektur in Großbritannien einem kosmopolitischen Schmelztiegel. Die in diesem Buch vorgestellten und überwiegend in der Hauptstadt ansässigen Architekten wurden in Bagdad, Daressalam, Shiraz, Madrid, in Zlin (Tschechien) oder Poole an der Südküste Englands geboren. Es ist nicht Anliegen dieses Buches, eine umfassende Bewertung der Architektur in Großbritannien vorzulegen, sondern eine Reihe unlängst entstandener Bauten vorzustellen, die gemeinsam eine Art Stimmungsbild der Situation im Jahr 2005 ergeben.

ES WAR EINMAL ...

Ganz gleich, wie groß die Zufuhr auswärtiger Kreativität in den Genpool der britischen Architektur auch sein mag, es bleibt dabei, dass das heutige Geschehen aus einer Tradition entstand. Ideenreichtum und gelegentliche Exzentrik sind nur ein Teil des hier herrschenden Geistes, wie ein Besuch der Räume mit englischer Malerei im Londoner Victoria & Albert Museum zeigt. Das heutige Bauen muss vor dem Hintergrund des Œuvres von Persönlichkeiten wie Alison und Peter Smithson, James Stirling, Cedric Price oder Archigram gesehen werden. So wird es nicht überraschen, dass es sich bei einer der neuesten und exotischsten Arbeiten eines englischen Architekten außerhalb Großbritanniens um ein Werk von Peter Cook, ehemals Mitglied von Archigram, handelt. Sein „friendly alien" (freundlicher Außerirdischer), ein biomorphes Gebilde, das im traditionell gesinnten Zentrum von Graz landete, ist das gemeinsam mit Colin Fournier entworfene neue Kunsthaus der Stadt. Andere Architekten sondierten emsig die Idee des „Blob" in der Architektur, aber nur wenige hätten gewagt, ein solch offenkundig amorphes Gebilde neben so viel altes Gestein und rote Ziegel zu stellen. James Stirling war mit Bauten wie seinem Leicester Engineering Building (1959–63) oder späteren

Arbeiten wie der Clore Gallery von Tate Britain in London tonangebend für die englische Kreativität in der jüngeren Vergangenheit. Mit einem Überraschungsefefekt wie ihn etwa eine purpurrote Tür in den Straßen Londons erzeugt, stellt Stirlings postmoderne Clore Gallery ein sehr britisches Farbempfinden zur Schau, indem die Farbe zutage tritt, wo man es am wenigsten erwartet und Besucher daran erinnert, dass unter der Oberfläche nicht alles so ruhig ist, wie es scheinen mag. In Yale, wo Stirling damals lehrte, trafen sich Norman Foster und Richard Rogers und gründeten kurz darauf ihre Partnerschaft Team 4. Wenngleich ein Großteil der Moderne vom Geist der Maschine beseelt war, gediehen gerade in England die fruchtbarsten Experimente mit mechanischen Formen, die in den Händen von Foster, Rogers und anderen die Bezeichnung „Hightech" erhielten. Die überraschenden Farben und Formen des Centre Georges Pompidou in Paris (Piano und Rogers, 1977) könnten kaum offensichtlichere Merkmale ihrer Abstammung tragen. Gleich einer Maschine, die ihr Innerstes nach Außen kehrt und für alle sichtbar ihre Rohre und Gewinde heraushängen lässt, oder einem deplatzierten, im alten Beaubourgviertel von Paris vor Anker gegangenen Flugzeugträger mutet das Centre Pompidou wie eine zum Leben erweckte Zeichnung von Archigram an. „Wir waren jung und wir wollten unbedingt kontrovers sein", gesteht ein etwas weiserer Renzo Piano heute. Rücksicht auf die umgebende Bebauung zählte nicht immer zu den Vorzügen zeitgenössischer Architektur in Großbritannien, wo man Brüche und Schockwirkungen häufig für die einzig möglichen Reaktionen auf Phlegma oder Schwerfälligkeit hielt. Natürlich stimmten nicht alle dieser Analyse zu. So zum Beispiel Denys Lasdun, der das National Theatre in London und ab 1962 einen Großteil der gewichtigen Architektur der University of East Anglia, Norwich, schuf. Großbritannien ist darüber hinaus das Land des Brutalismus, wo sich grauer Beton bisweilen traurig auf grauer Himmel reimt.

DIE LORDS DES HIGHTECH

Weil es sich bei ihnen um „Lords" im noblen britischen Wortsinn handelt, aber mehr noch, weil sie mit ihrer Architektur die heutige Landschaft so nachhaltig geprägt haben wie nur wenige andere, gebührt Richard Rogers und Norman Foster in jedem Überblick über die britische Architektur besondere Erwähnung. Das moderne London ist ebenso sehr von Rogers' Zentrale von Lloyd's of London (1978–86) geprägt wie von Fosters jüngerer Zentrale der Schweizer Rück (1997–2004). 1985 wurde Rogers die Goldmedaille des Royal Institute of British Architects und im Jahr 2000 der Praemium Imperiale zuerkannt. Zurzeit arbeitet er am Terminal 5 des Londoner Heathrow Airport (1989–2008) und am Sitz der National Assembly of Wales in Cardiff und bleibt damit seiner Hightech-Vergangenheit stärker verbunden als sein früherer Partner. Norman Foster, der 1983 mit der Royal Gold Medal for Architecture und 1994 mit der Goldmedaille des American Institute of Architects ausgezeichnet wurde, wandte seine methodische und innovative Auffassung von Materialien und Design bei unterschiedlichen Projekten an wie beim Flughafen Chek Lap Kok in Hongkong (1995–98), beim Umbau des Reichstagsgebäudes in Berlin (1995–99) oder bei der Neugestaltung des British Museum in London (1997–2000). Die Millennium Bridge (1996–2002), die zwischen St Paul's Cathedral und Tate Modern die Themse überquert, ist ebenso sein Entwurf wie die nahe gelegene Greater London Authority (1998–2002). Foster, der nicht nur von Materialien, sondern auch von Technik fasziniert ist, entwarf außerdem das gewaltige Grand Viaduc de Millau in Frankreich (1993–2005). Zu seiner Auffassung von Gestaltung und Materialien sagte Foster: „Ich beschäftige mich intensiv mit der äußeren Erscheinung, aber ich halte das Äußere nicht für eine Frage von Kosmetik. Ich glaube nicht, dass es viel damit zu tun hat, was es zum Frühstück gab oder auch nicht gab. Nur weil etwas gänzlich von Natur durchdrungen ist, ist es nicht automatisch schön. Auf der Hauptflugroute nach Heathrow können wir nach oben schauen und einige der hässlichsten Scheusale fliegen sehen. Andere sind absolut überwältigend. Das hat etwas mit der Art zu tun, wie die Designer die Kräfte und Druckverhältnisse interpretiert haben. Damit fängt es an. Es fängt nicht damit an, dass irgendjemand fragt, welche Sorte Flugzeug sollen wir heute bauen. Soll es eine Art Sopwith Camel, ein legendärer Doppeldecker aus dem Ersten Weltkrieg, werden?"

Der im Vergleich zu Foster und Rogers nur unwesentlich jüngere Nicholas Grimshaw ist ein weiterer innovativer britischer Architekt. Sein vermutlich bekanntestes Projekt ist das International Terminal am Londoner Bahnhof Waterloo (1988-93), das jeder mit dem Eurostar ankommende Reisende sieht. „Gute Detailarbeit steht an allererster Stelle, dann müssen Gebäude hinsichtlich ihres Raums und ihrer Gliederung verständlich gemacht werden", sagt Grimshaw, der diesen 400 m langen Anbau konzipierte. Bei diesem Gebäude, das Bezug nimmt auf das Vermächtnis von Ingenieuren und Architekten wie Joseph Paxton, Gustave Eiffel, Pierre Chareau und Jean Prouvé, ist ausnahmsweise Farbe Teil des Designs in Form leuchtend blauer Dachbinder. Eine vom Wendekreis der Züge und der Beschaffenheit des Geländes vorgegebene Bogenform veranlasste Grimshaw dazu, ein lockeres System sich überlappender Glasscheiben zu entwickeln, das viel Licht auf die Gleisanlage fallen lässt. „Einpassen", sagt Grimshaw, „hat mit Dingen wie Maßstab und Höhe, Licht und Schatten zu tun, dem Gefühl, das ein Gebäude im Erdgeschoss, auf der Ebene der Menschen vermittelt ... Es geht nicht darum, sich bloß dem Gebäude daneben anzupassen." Bei seinem Eden-Projekt in St Austell, Cornwall (1998-2005) stoßen Hightech und Ökologie zusammen und verbinden sich zu einem mit dem Begriff „Environment" treffend benannten Komplex.

Rücksicht auf die Umwelt spielt in der Berufspraxis von Michael Hopkins, einem weiteren Architekten aus der Generation von Rogers und Foster, eine wichtige Rolle. Nachdem er von 1968 bis 1976 mit Foster und dessen Frau Wendy zusammengearbeitet hatte, gewann Hopkins gemeinsam mit seiner Frau 1994 die Goldmedaille der RIBA. Hopkins bemerkt: „Seit unseren Anfängen 1976 haben wir eine Reihe von Verfahren neu eingeführt, darunter Dächer aus Textilwerkstoffen, Leichtbauweise, Energie sparende Entwürfe, das Einfügen neuer Bauten in bestehende Ensembles sowie Neunutzung von zuvor bereits bebautem Land." Hopkins, der wie seine Kollegen Foster, Grimshaw und Rogers in den 1930er Jahren geboren wurde, führte die Architektur in Großbritannien auf neue Höhen, indem er moderne Zielsetzungen in systematischer und innovativer Weise neu bestimmte und sich in zunehmendem Maß „grünen" Entwürfen widmete, die mit der ursprünglich technischen Ausrichtung keineswegs unvereinbar sind.

RITTER DER NÜCHTERNEN ELEGANZ

Obwohl es häufig künstlich anmutet, Architekten unter einem ästhetischen Schlagwort zusammenzufassen, scheint es doch offensichtlich, dass eine nach dem Krieg geborene Generation von Architekten neue Richtungen eingeschlagen hat,

die gegenwärtig das Aussehen des Bauens in Großbritannien und anderswo verändern. Der bekannteste von ihnen ist vielleicht David Chipperfield, der vor der Gründung seines eigenen Büros im Jahr 1984 bei Norman Foster und Richard Rogers tätig war. Obgleich er mit prestigeträchtigen, langfristigen Projekten wie dem Neuen Museum in Berlin (2000-09) oder dem Friedhof San Michele in Venedig (1998-2013) befasst ist, ist Chipperfields Arbeit durch die strengen Entwürfe des hier vorgestellten Ateliers von Antony Gormley in London (2001-03) gut vertreten. Chipperfield hat eine Reihe von Modeboutiquen gestaltet, aber aus seinen Entwürfen spricht mehr als nur schicker Minimalismus. Beim Atelier von Gormley gibt es eine sublimierte Anspielung auf Industriearchitektur und eine Funktionalität, die offenbaren, dass es sich hier um bedeutende Architektur handelt. Bei dieser Komposition in Grau und Weiß tritt die Architektur zurück, um der Kreativität des Bildhauers Antony Gormley den Vortritt zu lassen, sich selbst darzustellen. Dabei handelt es sich nicht um einen Ausdruck der Bescheidenheit, sondern vielmehr um wirkliches Verständnis vom Wesen der modernen Architektur.

Auch wenn die Architekturbüros David Adjaye und Caruso St John möglicherweise bewusst weniger zu minimalistischer Perfektion neigen als Chipperfield, pflegen sie doch eine reduzierte Nüchternheit, die mehr Subtilität und Intelligenz einsetzt als plumpe Extravaganz. Der 1966 geborene Adjaye arbeitete zu Beginn der 1990er Jahre im Büro von Chipperfield. Er ist einer der kommenden Stars der Architektur in Großbritannien, zum einen, weil er für berühmte Auftraggeber tätig war, zum anderen, weil er mit der Tradition gebrochen hat. Mit seinen neueren Arbeiten, darunter der „Idea Store", erforscht er die Kluft zwischen der Öffentlichkeit und einer intellektuellen Auffassung von Architektur und sagt: „Ich versuche eine Sprache des gegenseitigen Verstehens zwischen beiden Welten zu sprechen". Mit Arbeiten wie der radikalen Umnutzung eines früheren städtischen Parkhauses für die Gagosian Gallery nahe der U-Bahn-Station King's Cross hat das Büro von Caruso St John einen Sinn für praktische Anwendbarkeit bewiesen, obwohl die Architekten gleichzeitig den entschlossenen Willen zur Abschaffung alles Oberflächlichen an den Tag legen.

SPASS AN DER GRENZE

Man mag Peter Cooks „friendly alien" in Graz für verrückt halten, im Vergleich zu Will Alsops College of Art and Design in Toronto wirkt er harmlos. Offenbar angeregt vom Œuvre El Lissitzkys, gleicht es eher einem mit Anabolika behandelten Esstisch von Memphis. Der Entwurf mit einem „schwebenden Kasten" auf 29 m hohen Stelzen, in dem Unterrichtsräume untergebracht sind, wurde von der Stadt Toronto akzeptiert, obgleich er sich gänzlich außerhalb jeglicher vor Ort geltender architektonischer Normen bewegt. Der 1947 geborene Will Alsop arbeitete ebenfalls im Büro von Cedric Price (1973-77). Er behielt ein reges Interesse an Kunst, wie das 25 t schwere „konstruktive Geschlängel" deutlich beweist, das vom Dach des Ben Pimlott Gebäudes des Goldsmiths College (St James', New Cross, London, 2003-05) aufsteigt. Die Stornierung einiger Projekte Alsops führte kürzlich zu einer Neuordnung seines Büros, aber er ist nach wie vor davon überzeugt, dass die Architektur in Großbritannien nicht risikofreudig genug ist. Er erklärte freimütig: „Wir hatten bereits beschlossen, dass unsere Zukunft in Nordamerika, dem Fernen Osten und Moskau liegt, weil in unseren traditionellen Jagdgründen in Europa nicht viel passiert ..."

Es gibt natürlich auch Architekten, die ihre wahren kreativen Höhenflüge auf private Bauvorhaben beschränken. So etwa Laurie Chetwood, dessen Butterfly House zu einem völlig unerwarteten „Experiment einer architekturalen Skulptur " wurde. Die Inspiration zu diesem Projekt lieferte die sich stark vermehrende Schmetterlingspopulation in der Nähe eines von ihm erworbenen Hauses, das er in Anlehnung an die Farben und Formen der Insekten vollständig umgestaltete. Seinem Butterfly House kommt, obgleich auf grundsoliden Prinzipien basierend, eine Sonderstellung zu, die es auch im Vergleich mit den vielfältigen Spielarten der zeitgenössischen Architektur in Großbritannien mühelos behauptet. Laurie Chetwood ist der seltene Fall eines seriösen Architekten mit hohem professionellem Anspruch, der seiner Fantasie freien Lauf lässt. Sein Büro gewann im Jahr 2000 den „Practice of the Year"-Preis.

Chetwoods Butterfly House orientiert sich eindeutig an ökologischen Grundsätzen, allein schon wegen des „als perfektes Schmetterlingsbiotop" konzipierten Gartens. In Großbritannien haben viele andere Architekten Nachhaltigkeit und ähnliche „grüne" Themen auf andere Weise sondiert. Der 1931 in London geborene Edward Cullinan war von 1958 bis 1965 bei Denys Lasdun tätig und arbeitete damals speziell an den Studentenwohnheimen der University of East Anglia. Dieser Hintergrund ist insofern überraschend, als seine vor wenigen Jahren entstandene Downland Gridshell (Singleton, West Sussex, 2000–02) mit Merkmalen wie unbehandelten Holzböden, viel Tageslicht und der Nutzung von Erdwärme zur Regelung der Temperatur ernsthaftes Interesse an ökologischen Fragen erkennen lässt. Cullinan vertritt eine alternative Richtung in der zeitgenössischen Architektur, ohne irgendeinen beherrschenden Trend zu beachten. Er ist eine einfallsreiche, faszinierende Persönlichkeit.

MEISTER DES UMBAUENS
Für das Umgestalten alter Gebäude, seien es Wohn- oder Industriebauten, um ihnen zu moderner Anmutung und Funktionalität zu verhelfen, wird es in der zeitgenössischen Architektur offenkundig lang anhaltenden Bedarf geben. Obgleich sie sich nicht wirklich auf Umbauten spezialisiert haben, waren Eva Jiricna und Dominic Williams auf unterschiedliche Weise besonders erfolgreich, wenn es darum ging, vorhandenen Bauten neues Leben einzuhauchen. Jiricna, die für die Innenarchitektur der Zentrale von Lloyd's zuständig war, verfügt damit gewiss über gute Referenzen als moderne Designerin. Sie hat Boutiquen für Hugo Boss, Joseph und Joan & David gestaltet und dabei häufig ungewöhnliche, skulpturale Treppen geschaffen. Williams übernahm die schmutzigere Arbeit, als er eine alte industrielle Getreidemühle in ein Museum verwandelte (Baltic Centre for Contemporary Art, Newcastle, 1999–2002).

FRAUEN GANZ OBEN
Neben Eva Jiricna handelt es sich bei den beiden anderen in diesem Buch vorgestellten Frauen eindeutig um international führende Persönlichkeiten. Vielleicht ist es nur Zufall, dass beide aus dem Mittleren Osten stammen. Zaha Hadid muss man kaum vorstellen, seit sie 2004 mit dem Pritzker Prize ausgezeichnet wurde, ist sie eine bekannte Größe. Sie war die erste Frau, die diesen renommierten Preis, der zum dritten Mal nach Großbritannien ging, erhalten hatte. Sie folgte einem von Architekten wie ihrem früheren Partner bei OMA, Rem Koolhaas, eingeführten Beispiel, indem sie sich mit theoretischen oder genauer visuell orientierten Planungen eine respektable Reputation erwarb. Ihr Zeichenstil fand Beachtung und hatte großen Anteil an wichtigen Ausstellungen wie der Schau „Deconstructivist Architecture" am MoMA in New York. Zaha Hadid gelang ein nahtloser Übergang von ungebauten Planungen zu wichtigen Bauten, wenngleich sich ihre bedeutendsten Werke, wie das vor wenigen Jahren entstandene Rosenthal Center for Contemporary Art in Cincinatti, Ohio (1999–2003), und das Zentralgebäude der Fertigungsanlage für BMW in Leipzig (2005), außerhalb Großbritanniens befinden.

Farshi Moussavi von Foreign Office Architects (FOA) ist noch nicht annähernd so bekannt wie Zaha Hadid, aber mit ihrem Partner, Alejandro Zaera Polo, ist auch sie dabei, Formen und Methoden der zeitgenössischen Architektur neu zu definieren. 1988 war sie in Genua für den Renzo Piano Building Workshop tätig und von 1991 bis 1993 für Rem Koolhaas' Office of Metropolitan Architecture in Rotterdam, während sie 1992 FOA begründete. Mit dem Yokohama International Port Terminal (2000–02) erschloss das Büro beinahe im Wortsinn Neuland. Zu diesem Thema schreiben die Architekten: „Statt das Gebäude als Objekt oder Symbol auf dem Pier zu gestalten, wurde das Projekt als Erweiterung des städtischen Bodens konzipiert, ausgearbeitet als systematische Umwandlung der Linien der Erschließungssysteme zu einer gefalteten, gegabelten Oberfläche. Der gefaltete Boden verteilt die Lasten durch die Oberflächen selbst, indem er sie in diagonaler Richtung zum Boden bewegt."

Die in Shiraz im Iran geborene Moussavi vertritt, ebenso wie Hadid, insofern eine andere Art von Architektenschaft, als sie sich zunehmend weniger einer lokalen Identität verpflichtet fühlt. Nur wenige würden Zaha Hadid als irakische Architektin beschreiben, aber ebenso wenige fänden ihr Œuvre spezifisch englisch. Dies soll nicht heißen, dass Globetrotter wie Foster oder Hadid einer Lösung sämtlicher Probleme der zeitgenössischen Architektur nach Art eines „globalisierten" Quodlibets das Wort reden. Tatsächlich gehen sie besonders einfühlsam auf die Bedürfnisse eines bestimmten Ortes ein, egal um welches Land es sich handelt. Natürlich verfügt heute weder jeder Architekt über den Hintergrund und die nötigen Mittel, um einer internationalen Karriere gewachsen zu sein, noch hat er überhaupt den Wunsch dazu. Computergestütztes Entwerfen und Kommunizieren erleichtert entscheiden die Arbeit von Architekten wie Hadid und Moussavi, und ihre Präsenz in London verändert die früher dem Architektenberuf zugeordneten Definitionen. Zum Glück wird es immer Architekten geben, die es vorziehen, eine rein lokale Identität zu pflegen, aber London ist heute Standort einiger der wichtigsten, internationalen Architekten, und dies wird sich wohl in naher Zukunft kaum ändern.

Philip Jodidio

INTRODUCTION

LE COMBAT DANS L'ÎLE

La couverture d'un récent magazine espagnol sur l'architecture britannique contemporaine faisait presque penser à une publicité pour *La Guerre des mondes*. Les austères formes blanches et grises de l'atelier londonien d'Antony Gormley par David Chipperfield, les volumes improbables du grand magasin Selfridge's à Birmingham par Future Systems et ceux du College of Art and Design de Will Alsop à Toronto semblaient se livrer à une bataille féroce sur quelque territoire résolument insulaire. Si ce photomontage espagnol n'avançait aucun pronostic sur le vainqueur, il mettait le doigt sur la remarquable diversité actuelle de l'architecture contemporaine au Royaume-Uni. Même si quelques prestigieux praticiens basés à Londres, de Lord Norman Foster à Zaha Hadid en passant par Foreign Office Architects, réalisent leurs œuvres les plus importantes loin de la Tamise, un bref survol de la construction britannique récente montre un éventail de solutions qui vont de la rigueur minimaliste aux excès pop. Peu d'autres pays ont réussi à gérer simultanément l'influence de traditions séculaires révérées et celle de groupes musicaux comme les Sex Pistols. Les contrastes frappants et les approches esthétiques en divergence radicale sont peut-être simplement un signe des temps. Le couturier britannique John Galliano a foulé aux pieds le style établi de Christian Dior, tout en redonnant un lustre nouveau à une marque un peu fatiguée. Serait-il une source d'inspiration pour les architectes ? Si le design anglais triomphe à l'étranger, jusqu'à quel point est-il encore insulaire ? Dans l'image de la capitale elle-même, on peut constater que l'architecture contemporaine est le fruit d'un melting-pot cosmopolite. Les architectes présentés dans ce livre, installés pour la plupart à Londres, ne sont-ils pas nés à Bagdad, Dar Es-Salaam, Shiraz, Madrid, Zlin (République Tchèque) ou Poole dans le Dorset ? L'objectif de cet ouvrage n'est pas de donner une évaluation exhaustive de l'architecture en Grande-Bretagne, mais de présenter une sélection d'un certain nombre de réalisations très récentes qui, toutes réunies, offrent un baromètre assez précis de la situation en 2005.

IL ÉTAIT UNE FOIS...

Quelle que soit l'importance du niveau de créativité étrangère insufflé dans la banque de gènes de l'architecture britannique, il reste que ce qui se produit ici est issu d'une tradition. L'inventivité et l'excentricité occasionnelles font vraiment partie du contexte, comme le montre une visite des galeries anglaises du Victoria & Albert Museum. Le travail actuel doit être considéré avec, pour toile de fond, l'œuvre de prédécesseurs comme Alison et Peter Smithson, James Stirling, Cedric Price ou Archigram. Il n'est pas surprenant que l'une des réalisations britanniques récentes hors du Royaume-Uni qui ait le plus étonné soit le fait de Peter Cook, un ancien d'Archigram. Son « extra-terrestre amical », bulbeuse créature lâchée en plein cœur de la très traditionnelle Graz (Autriche), est en fait une nouvelle Kunsthaus municipale (conçue en collaboration avec Colin Fournier). D'autres architectes ont activement exploré le concept de « blob » en architecture, mais peu d'entre eux auraient osé juxtaposer un exercice de style apparemment informel au beau milieu d'un environnement de pierres et de tuiles rouges. James Stirling, à travers des œuvres comme le bâtiment de Leicester Engineerings (1959–63), ou plus tard la Clore Gallery à la Tate Britain de Londres, a fortement donné le ton à la créativité britannique au cours de ces dernières années. Telle une de ces portes rouge vif que l'on remarque parfois dans les rues de Londres, la Clore Gallery d'es-

prit postmoderne témoigne d'un sens très anglais de la couleur surgissant là où on l'attend le moins, et rappelant aux visiteurs que sous la surface tout n'est peut-être pas aussi calme qu'il y paraît. C'est à Yale, où Stirling enseignait alors, que Norman Foster et Richard Rogers se rencontrèrent avant de créer peu après leur agence Team 4. Bien qu'une bonne partie du mouvement moderne se soit inspiré de l'esprit de la machine, c'est en Grande-Bretagne que furent menées les expérimentations les plus fructueuses sur les formes mécaniques, aboutissant à ce qui allait devenir le style « High Tech » entre les mains de Rogers, Foster et quelques autres. Les formes et les couleurs étonnantes du Centre Pompidou à Paris (Piano et Rogers, 1977) ne pouvaient afficher plus clairement leur paternité. Comme une machine retournée vers l'extérieur avec ses tubes et échelles apparentes, improbable machine volante atterrie en plein Paris dans le vieux quartier de Beaubourg, le Centre était pratiquement un projet d'Archigram pour une fois réalisé. « Nous étions jeunes et nous voulions vraiment choquer... » confie aujourd'hui un Renzo Piano assagi. Le contextualisme n'a pas toujours été une qualité de l'architecture contemporaine au Royaume-Uni, où la rupture et la surprise ont souvent été la seule réponse à l'immobilisme ou à la lourdeur. Naturellement tout le monde ne s'est pas rallié à cette analyse. Par exemple, il ne faudrait pas oublier Denys Lasdun qui a conçu le National Theatre à Londres et une bonne partie des pesants bâtiments de l'Université d'East Anglia, Norwich, à partir de 1962. Le Royaume-Uni est aussi la terre du brutalisme où béton gris rime tristement avec ciel gris.

LES SEIGNEURS DES TECHNIQUES

Parce qu'ils sont des lords au sens de l'aristocratie anglaise mais surtout parce que leur architecture a davantage marqué le paysage contemporain que celle de beaucoup de leurs contemporains, Richard Rogers et Norman Foster méritent une attention spéciale dans ce survol. Le panorama du Londres moderne doit beaucoup au siège des Lloyd's par Rogers (1978–86) et au très récent siège de Swiss Re par Foster publié ici (1997–2004). Titulaire de la médaille d'or du RIBA 1985 et du Praemium Imperiale 2000, travaillant actuellement sur le terminal 5 de l'aéroport londonien d'Heathrow (1989–2008), et l'Assemblée nationale du Pays de Galles à Cardiff, Rogers demeure une référence internationale, mais reste davantage lié à son passé high-tech que son ancien associé. Titulaire de la médaille d'or royale pour l'architecture (1983) et de la médaille d'or de l'American Institute of Architects (1994), Lord Norman Foster a appliqué son approche novatrice et méthodique des matériaux et de la conception à des projets aussi variés que l'aéroport de Chep Lap Kok (Honkong, 1995–98), le Reichstag (Berlin, 1995–99) ou la restructuration du British Museum (Londres, 1997–2000). Le Millenium Bridge (1996–2002) qui franchit la Tamise entre la cathédrale Saint-Paul et la Tate Modern est également son œuvre de même que l'immeuble de la Greater London Authority (1998–2002). Fasciné à la fois par les matériaux et l'ingénierie, il a également conçu le gigantesque viaduc de Millau en France (1993–2005). Il définit ainsi son approche : « Je me préoccupe intensément de l'apparence, mais je ne pense pas que celle-ci relève du cosmétique. Je ne pense pas que cela a voir avec ce que j'ai pu consommer à mon petit déjeuner. Cela ne veut pas dire qu'un bâtiment totalement construit en fonction de la nature sera automatiquement beau. Sur la piste principale d'Heathrow, on voit en levant la tête quelques monstres s'envoler. Certains sont absolument bouleversants. C'est dû à la façon dont leurs concepteurs ont interprété certaines forces, certaines pressions. C'est là que tout commence. Les choses ne débutent pas par quelqu'un qui dirait, « Tiens, quel type d'avion allons-nous avoir aujourd'hui...? »

Légèrement plus jeune que Foster et Rogers, Nicholas Grimshaw est lui aussi l'un de ces architectes anglais innovants fascinés par la technologie. Son œuvre la plus célèbre est certainement le terminal international de la gare de Waterloo à Londres (1988–93) que connaît tout voyageur de l'Eurostar. « La qualité de la réalisation vient en premier. Ensuite, il faut que le bâtiment soit compréhensible, spatialement et sur le plan de son organisation », précise Grimshaw qui a conçu cette extension de 400 m de long d'une gare historique. La couleur y joue un rôle exceptionnel sous forme de poutres métalliques bleu vif pour une voûte transparente qui évoque les travaux d'ingénieurs ou architectes comme Joseph Paxton, Gustave Eiffel, Pierre Chareau et Jean Prouvé. La forme incurvée imposée par le rayon de virage des trains et la nature du site ont poussé Grimshaw à imaginer une couverture et des parois en panneaux de verre superposés « d'adaptation souple » qui diffusent un éclairage naturel généreux. « S'adapter », dit-il « est en rapport avec des choses comme l'échelle et la hauteur, la lumière et l'ombre, le sentiment que le bâtiment donne au niveau du sol, au niveau du visiteur... ce n'est pas seulement penser au bâtiment d'à côté. » Son Eden Project (St Austell, Cornouailles, 1998–2005), publié ici, est un remarquable croisement de high-tech et d'approche écologique volontariste pour créer un environnement qui porte bien son nom d'éden.

Les préoccupations écologiques sont un point fort de la pratique d'un autre architecte de la génération de Foster et Rogers, Michael Hopkins. Après avoir travaillé avec Foster et son épouse-associée Wendy de 1968 à 1976, Hopkins a remporté la médaille d'or du RIBA en 1994 en compagnie de la sienne. « Quand nous avons débuté en 1976, nous avons exploré une série de stratégies dont des toits en toile, des structures légères, des techniques d'économie d'énergie, l'imbrication de constructions nouvelles dans des bâtiments anciens et le recyclage de friches industrielles. » Comme ses confrères nés dans les années 1930, Hopkins a porté l'architecture britannique à de nouveaux sommets, en redéfinissant les objectifs du modernisme de façon systématique et novatrice, et en évoluant de plus en plus vers une approche « verte » qui n'est en rien incompatible avec son orientation technologique initiale.

LE NOUVEAU CHIC ANGLAIS
Bien qu'il soit souvent artificiel de regrouper des architectes sous une même bannière esthétique, il semble clair qu'une nouvelle génération de praticiens, née après la guerre, se soit engagée dans de nouvelles orientations qui modifient l'aspect de ce qui se construit actuellement en Grande-Bretagne et dans le monde. Le plus connu d'entre eux est probablement David Chipperfield qui a travaillé dans les agences de Norman Foster et de Richard Rogers avant de créer sa propre structure en 1984. Bien qu'il soit lancé dans de lourds projets à long terme et de haute visibilité comme le Neues Museum (Berlin, 2000–09) ou le cimetière de San Michele (Venise, 1998–2013), son œuvre est particulièrement bien illustrée par la rigueur de l'atelier d'Antony Gormley (Londres, 2001–03), publié ici. Même s'il a conçu un certain nombre de boutiques de mode, le minimalisme chic n'est

qu'une des composantes de son travail. Dans le cas du Gormley Studio, on remarque une référence sublimée à l'architecture industrielle et une fonctionnalité qui signifie clairement que l'on est vraiment en présence d'une architecture sérieuse. Dans cette composition en gris et blanc, l'architecture reste en retrait pour permettre à la créativité du sculpteur Gormley de s'exprimer en toute liberté. C'est moins une déclaration de modestie qu'une compréhension profonde de la nature même de l'architecture moderne.

Bien qu'ils soient peut-être moins attachés à la perfection minimaliste que Chipperfield, les architectes David Adjaye et Caruso St John pratiquent tous deux une austérité épurée qui joue sur la subtilité et l'intelligence, plus que sur l'extravagance appuyée. Adjaye, né en 1966, qui a travaillé chez Chipperfield au début des années 1990, est une des étoiles montantes de l'architecture au Royaume-Uni, en partie parce qu'il a travaillé pour des clients célèbres, mais aussi pour sa rupture avec les conventions. Travaillant pour ses réalisations récentes, dont l'Idea Store publiée ici, dans un entre-deux conceptuel entre le style de la rue et une approche intellectuelle de l'architecture, il explique : « J'essaye de parler un langage de compréhension mutuelle entre ces deux mondes. » Avec des interventions comme la rénovation radicale d'un ancien garage municipal près de la gare de Kings Cross pour la Gagosian Gallery, Caruso St John ont prouvé leur sens du fonctionnel même lorsqu'ils affichent une volonté rigoureuse d'éliminer le superficiel.

ON SAIT ENCORE SE FAIRE PLAISIR
Aussi incroyable « l'extra-terrestre amical » de Peter Cook à Graz puisse-t-il sembler, il pâlit en comparaison avec le College d'Art and Design de Toronto par Will Alsop. Apparemment inspiré par l'œuvre d'El Lissitzky, il fait davantage penser à une table de Memphis sous stéroïdes. Cette « boîte en suspension » posée sur des pilotis de 29 m de haut et qui contient les salles de cours a été acceptée par la ville de Toronto bien qu'à l'écart de toute norme architecturale locale. Né en 1947, Alsop a travaillé dans l'agence de Cedric Price (1973–77) et s'est toujours activement intéressé à l'art, comme le montre son « gribouillis structurel » de 25 tonnes qui jaillit du sommet de l'immeuble Ben Pimlott (St James', New Cross, Londres, 2003–05) du Goldsmith College publié dans ces pages. Si l'annulation récente de certaines commandes de l'architecte a conduit à une réorganisation de son agence, il reste convaincu que l'architecture en Grande-Bretagne ne prend pas assez de risques et a déclaré : « Nous avons déjà décidé que notre futur se trouvait du côté de l'Amérique du Nord, en Extrême-Orient et à Moscou, car il ne se passe vraiment pas grand-chose sur nos terrains de chasse européens traditionnels... »

Certains architectes limitent leur fantaisie à des œuvres moins publiques et moins visibles. C'est le cas de Laurie Chestwood, dont la Maison Papillon est une étonnante « expérimentation en sculpture architecturale. » Inspiré par la prolifération de papillons près d'une maison qu'il avait achetée, il l'a entièrement remodelée à partir de la forme et des couleurs de ces insectes. Bien qu'elle prenne appui sur des bases fondées, cette maison se détache de la très grande variété des projets contemporains britanniques. C'est un des rares cas de praticien sérieux et professionnel dont l'agence a remporté le prix de « L'Agence de l'année » 2000 tout en laissant totalement la bride sur le cou à son imagination.

Cette maison est d'orientation écologique évidente, ne serait-ce que parce que le jardin est « conçu comme un habitat parfait pour les papillons ». Mais beaucoup d'architectes au Royaume-Uni ont exploré l'axe du développement durable et les préoccupations « vertes » d'autres façons. Edward Cullinan, né à Londres en 1931, a travaillé auprès de Denys Lasdun (1958-65) et en particulier sur les logements pour étudiants de l'Université d'East Anglia ce qui ne laisse pas de surprendre lorsque l'on découvre aujourd'hui son très récent Downland Gridshell (Singleton, West Sussex, 2000-02) qui témoigne d'un souci authentique de l'écologie en faisant appel, par exemple, à des sols en bois non traités, à une généreuse lumière naturelle et à la masse thermique du sol pour contrôler la température. Par-dessus tout, Cullinan représente une orientation différente et ouverte de l'architecture contemporaine, sans se soucier d'une quelconque tendance dominante. C'est un personnage inventif et particulièrement intéressant.

LE MAQUILLAGE EST UN ART
Apporter la modernité et un fonctionnalisme authentiques à des bâtiments anciens, qu'ils soient résidentiels ou industriels, est certainement un besoin actuel qui possède un bel avenir devant lui. Bien que ni l'un ni l'autre ne soient spécialisés dans les reconversions, Eva Jiricna et Dominic Williams de l'agence Ellis Williams ont particulièrement réussi, chacun à sa façon, à insuffler une vie nouvelle à des bâtiments existants. Jiricna est une praticienne confirmée, qui affiche à son palmarès les aménagements intérieurs du siège des Lloyds. Elle a conçu des magasins Hugo Boss, Joseph ou Joan & David pour lesquels elle a souvent créé de spectaculaires escaliers sculpturaux. Williams, lui, a pris en charge le projet plus « salissant » de transformer un ancien moulin industriel en musée (Baltic Centre for Contemporary Arts, Newcastle, 1999-2002). Né en 1965, Dominic Williams a travaillé pour Skidmore, Owings and Merrill (1991-94), avant de fonder Ellis Williams Partnership en 1994. Il représente une génération plus jeune, sensible à des enjeux qui vont des relations entre l'art et l'architecture aux préoccupations écologiques.

FEMMES AU SOMMET
Bien que l'architecture britannique ait longtemps été un bastion masculin, deux femmes sélectionnées pour cet ouvrage sont devenues des célébrités internationales. Toutes deux par coïncidence sont nées au Moyen-Orient. Zaha Hadid n'a plus à être présentée, en particulier après qu'elle ait reçu le Pritzker Prize en 2004. En plus d'être la première femme titulaire de ce prix prestigieux, elle est la troisième architecte basée au Royaume-Uni, après James Stirling en 1981 et Norman Foster en 1999 à l'avoir remporté, ce qui la met en bonne compagnie. Suivant un parcours balisé par des architectes comme Rem Koolhaas, dont elle fut associée dans OMA, elle s'est fait une réputation considérable par ses propositions théoriques ou plus précisément orientées sur les visuels. Son style de dessin remarqué lui avait valu d'être retenue pour d'importantes expositions comme celle de « Deconstructivist Architecture » au MoMA de New York. Elle a réussi une transition délicate entre projets et réalisation, même si ses œuvres les plus importantes, comme le récent Rosenthal Center for Contemporary Art (Cincinnati, Ohio, 1999-2003) et le bâtiment central de l'usine BMW de Leipzig (2005), ont été construites loin de la Grande-Bretagne.

Farshid Moussavi de Foreign Office Architects n'est pas aussi connue que Zaha Hadid, mais avec son partenaire Alejandro Zaera Polo, elle contribue elle aussi à la redéfinition des formes et approches de l'architecture contemporaine. Elle a travaillé pour Renzo Piano à Gênes en 1988 et pour OMA à Rotterdam (Rem Koolhaas, 1991-93) tout en créant l'agence FOA en 1992. Le terminal international du port de Yokohama réalisé par le couple et abondamment reproduit (Yokohama, Japon, 2000-02) créait littéralement de nouvelles bases. Comme ils l'ont expliqué : « Plutôt qu'un bâtiment qui soit un objet posé sur une jetée, le projet est une extension de la ville, élaborée comme une transformation systématique des axes du plan de circulation en une surface pliée et bifurquée ... le sol plié distribue les charges par l'intermédiaire des surfaces elles-mêmes, les déplaçant en diagonale par rapport au sol. »

Née à Shiraz en Iran, Farshid Moussavi comme Zaha Hadid est représentative d'une autre génération d'architectes, de moins en moins liée à une identité locale spécifique. Z. Hadid est rarement qualifiée d'architecte irakienne, mais son œuvre n'est pas davantage typiquement britannique. Ceci ne veut pas dire que des globetrotters comme Foster ou Hadid proposent des solutions attrape-tout « globalisées ». Ils sont en fait particulièrement sensibles aux besoins du site, quel que soit le pays. Tous les architectes n'ont pas pour autant la formation et les moyens financiers de mener une carrière vraiment internationale, sans parler du désir de le faire. La CAO et les technologies de la communication facilitent certainement la tâche de gens comme Hadid ou Moussavi et leur présence à Londres transforme les définitions retenues jusqu'alors pour la profession architecturale. Heureusement, il restera toujours des praticiens attachés à une identité purement locale, mais il reste que Londres est aujourd'hui le port d'attache de certains des architectes qui comptent le plus dans le monde, situation qui n'est sans doute pas prête de changer.

Philip Jodidio

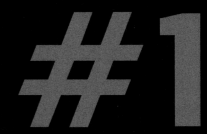

DAVID ADJAYE

ADJAYE/ASSOCIATES
23–28 Penn Street
London N1 5DL

Tel: +44 20 77 39 49 69
Fax: +44 20 77 39 34 84
e-mail: info@adjaye.com
Web: www.adjaye.com

DAVID ADJAYE was born in 1966 in Dar-Es-Salaam, Tanzania. He studied at the Royal College of Art (Masters in Architecture, 1993), and worked in the offices of David Chipperfield and Eduardo Souto de Moura before creating his own firm in London in 2000 (Chassay Architects, 1988–90; David Chipperfield Architects, 1991; Eduardo Souto de Moura Architects, 1991; Adjaye & Russell, 1994–2000). He has been widely recognized as one of the leading architects of his generation in the UK, in part because of the talks he has given in various locations, such as the Architectural Association (AA) in London, the Royal College of Art, London, and Cambridge University, as well as Harvard, Cornell, and the Universidad de Luisdad in Lisbon. He was also the co-presenter of the BBC's six-part series on modern architecture, "Dreamspaces." His Idea Store library in East London (featured here) was selected by Deyan Sudjic for the exhibition highlighting 100 projects that are changing the world at the 8th Venice Biennale of Architecture in 2002. His offices currently employ a staff of 35, and some of his key works are: Studio/home for Chris Ofili, London (1999); Extension to house, St John's Wood (1998); Siefert Penthouse, London (2001); Elektra House, London (2001); Studio/gallery/home for Tim Noble and Sue Webster, London (2002); and the SHADA Pavilion, London (2000, with artist Henna Nadeem). Current work includes: The Nobel Peace Center, Oslo (2002–05); Bernie Grant Performing Arts Centre, Tottenham, London (2001–06); Stephen Lawrence Centre, Deptford, London (2004–06); a visual arts building for the London-based organizations inIVA/Autograph, and the Museum of Contemporary Art, Denver, Colorado (2004–06).

IDEA STORE
CHRISP STREET
LONDON
2000 - 04

FLOOR AREA: 1034 m^2
CLIENT: London Borough of Tower Hamlets
COST: £137 300

Libraries have had a hard time of it, outpaced by the Internet, outmoded in their presentation and access in many parts of the world. The discovery that only 20 percent of its citizens ever went into a public library led the London area of Tower Hamlets, near Canary Wharf, to call on David Adjaye in the hope of creating new, more attractive facilities, after a competition in June 2001. To replace the worn-out stylistic vocabulary of public libraries, rejected by younger people and those familiar with more flamboyant retail spaces, David Adjaye used doors that open automatically, escalators and distinctive lighting or furniture to make the experience more fashionable and in tune with what is happening in shops or boutiques, for example. Tower Hamlets decided to close existing libraries and to replace them with seven "Idea Stores" located in central shopping areas that include a cafe, adult education classes and computer access. Adjaye's first Idea Store, on Chrisp Street, seeks to break down the barriers between the library and the street, and features colored glazing that serves as a distinctive signal. The blue and green stripes of the building are intended to bring to mind spines of books. Its steel shed structure is placed on top of existing shops and reaches down to street level near its entrance. As David Adjaye says, "What's really clear is that the human condition has produced a series of inhabited spaces that are very specific, that are about a clash of ideas, the ideas of objective truth and massive force-driven systems. And I'm fascinated by the fissure between these two things. And I'm not trying to repair, but I'm trying to speak a language of mutual understanding between both worlds. I'm ultimately bored by one language over the other, and I'm completely interested in the polyvalence of all the languages kind of working at the same time. You could say that that makes a really bad din, but I think architecture is not noise. Actually it makes really beautiful forms."

Überholt vom Internet und in Bezug auf Präsentation und Verfügbarkeit oft veraltet, haben Bibliotheken es in vielen Teilen der Welt nicht leicht. Die Feststellung, dass nur 20 % der Bewohner je eine öffentliche Bibliothek betreten, veranlasste den in der Nähe von Canary Wharf gelegenen Londoner Bezirk Tower Hamlets dazu, sich nach einem Wettbewerb im Juni 2001 an David Adjaye zu wenden, in der Hoffnung, er werde eine neue, attraktivere Einrichtung schaffen. Anstelle der traditionellen Formensprache öffentlicher Bibliotheken, die von jungen Leuten und einer Klientel, die mit pompöseren Verkaufsräumen vertraut ist, abgelehnt wird, verwendete David Adjaye Türen, die sich automatisch öffnen, prägnante Beleuchtungskörper und Möbel sowie Rolltreppen, um das Erlebnis moderner und der Einrichtung von Läden oder Boutiquen ähnlicher zu gestalten. Die Bezirksverwaltung beschloss, die vorhandenen Bibliotheken zu schließen und sie durch sieben in zentralen Einkaufsgebieten gelegene „Idea Stores" zu ersetzen, die außerdem über ein Café verfügen und Kurse in Erwachsenenbildung anbieten. Mit seinem ersten Idea Store in der Chrisp Street versucht Adjaye, die Barrieren zwischen Bibliothek und Straßenraum zu überwinden und setzt farbige Verglasung als charakteristisches Merkmal ein. Die blauen und grünen Glasstreifen der Fassade sollen an Bücherrücken erinnern. Mit dem an eine stählerne Lagerhalle erinnernden Gebäude wurden vorhandene Ladengeschäfte überbaut; nahe dem Eingang reicht die Gebäudefront bis auf das Straßenniveau herunter. David Adjaye meint dazu: „Wirklich klar ist, dass die menschliche Natur eine Reihe von spezifischen bewohnten Räumen geschaffen hat, bei denen ganz verschiedene Vorstellungen zusammenprallen: objektive Wahrheiten und fremdbestimmte Systeme. Und mich fasziniert der Gegensatz zwischen diesen beiden Polen. Und ich versuche nicht, etwas wiederherzustellen, sondern ich versuche, eine Sprache des gegenseitigen Verständnisses zwischen beiden Welten zu entwickeln. Letzten Endes langweilt es mich, wenn eine Sprache die Oberhand behält. Ich bin sehr daran interessiert, dass alle Sprachen gleichzeitig funktionieren. Man könnte meinen, daraus entstünde ein ziemlich schrecklicher Krach, aber ich glaube, Architektur hat nichts mit Geräusch zu tun. Tatsächlich lässt sie wirklich schöne Formen entstehen."

Dépassées par Internet, démodées dans leur style et leur mode d'accès, les bibliothèques traversent une période difficile un peu partout dans le monde. La découverte que 20 % seulement de ses administrés se rendaient de temps en temps dans une bibliothèque a conduit la municipalité de Tower Hamlets, près de Canary Wharf, à faire appel à David Adjaye à l'issue d'un concours organisé en juin 2001 afin de créer un équipement plus attirant. À la place du vocabulaire stylistique dépassé des bibliothèques publiques rejeté par les jeunes et les familiers d'espace commerciaux plus flamboyants, Adjaye a fait appel à des portes automatiques, des escalators et des systèmes d'éclairage du mobilier pour rendre la perception du lieu plus contemporaine, dans l'esprit, entre autres, de ce que l'on peut trouver dans les magasins et les boutiques. Tower Hamlets décida de fermer ses bibliothèques existantes et de les remplacer par sept « Idea Stores » situées dans les zones commerciales et intégrant un café, des installations d'enseignement pour adultes et l'accès à des ordinateurs. La première Idea Store d'Adjaye sur Chrisp Street cherche à supprimer les barrières entre la bibliothèque et la rue et se signale par une façade en verre coloré. Les bandes verticales bleues et blanches de la façade rappellent des reliures de livres. La structure en acier de type shed s'élève au-dessus des commerces existants mais descend jusqu'au niveau de la rue dans la zone de l'entrée. Comme David Adjaye l'explique : « Ce qui est très clair est que la condition humaine a produit une série d'espaces inhabités très spécifiques, qui représentent un affrontement d'idées, des idées de vérité objective et de systèmes dotés d'une puissance massive. Et je suis fasciné par la faille entre ces deux choses. Je n'essaye pas de réparer quoi que ce soit, mais je tente de parler un langage de compréhension mutuelle entre ces deux mondes. Qu'un langage domine un autre m'ennuie, je m'intéresse totalement à la polyvalence de toutes les sortes de langages s'exprimant ensemble. On pourrait penser que cela fait beaucoup de tapage, mais je crois que l'architecture doit être un bruit. En fait, cela aboutit à des formes réellement magnifiques. »

The Idea Store looks more like an upscale fashion or design shop than it does a typical local library, and both architects and town officials are apparently counting on this factor to change public perceptions.

Der Idea Store gleicht eher einem exklusiven Mode- oder Designladen als einer typischen Stadtbibliothek. Offenbar rechnen die Architekten und auch die Vertreter der Stadt damit, dass die Wahrnehmung der Öffentlichkeit sich auf diese Weise ändert.

L'Idea Store fait davantage penser à un magasin de mode ou de design haut de gamme qu'à une bibliothèque de quartier. Les architectes et les autorités locales comptent précisément sur ce facteur pour modifier la perception du public.

The long, low volume of the structure is contrasted with the colorful vertical glass cladding. Floor plans show the curving book stacks on the upper level, and the overall slight irregularity of the shape of the building.

Der lang gezogene, flache Baukörper kontrastiert mit der bunten, vertikalen Verglasung. Die Grundrisse zeigen die gebogenen Bücherregale im Obergeschoss und die leichte Unregelmäßigkeit der Gebäudeform.

Le volume long et bas de la construction contraste avec son habillage en panneaux verticaux de verre de couleur. Les plans montrent l'implantation des rayonnages de livres sinueux au niveau supérieur et la légère irrégularité générale de la forme du bâtiment.

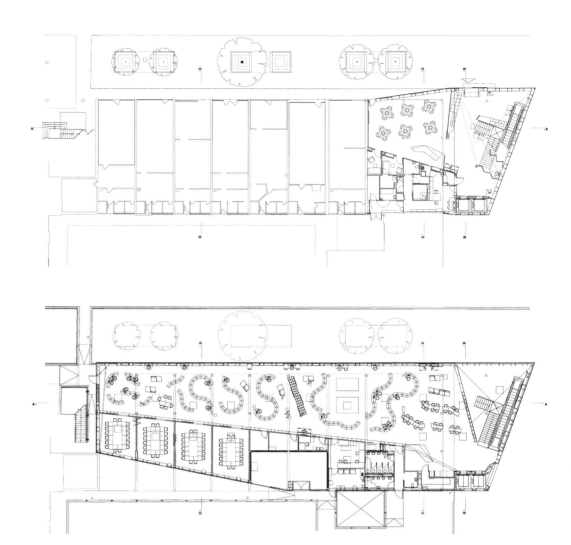

The interiors are colorful, bright and open. To the right, the "Surfing Space" offers computer access. Adjaye uses a modern and yet certainly not minimalist vocabulary to heighten the spatial interest of the Idea Store.

Die Innenräume sind bunt, hell und offen. Das „Surfing Space" rechts bietet Zugang zu Computer-Arbeitsplätzen. Um die Räume des Idea Store interessant zu gestalten, bedient sich Adjaye einer modernen, jedoch keineswegs minimalistischen Formensprache.

Les aménagements intérieurs sont colorés, lumineux et ouverts. À droite, le « Surfing Space » est réservé à l'Internet. Adjaye utilise un vocabulaire moderne qui n'est certainement pas minimaliste pour renforcer l'intérêt spatial de l'Idea Store.

IDEA STORE WHITECHAPEL
LONDON 2001 - 05

FLOOR AREA: 4459 m²
CLIENT: London Borough of Tower Hamlets
COST: £11.3 million

Larger than the Chrisp Street facility, the new Whitechapel Idea Store uses the same curtain wall "with a repeating pattern of colored glass, clear glass, and glass faced aluminum panels enclose all four facades." A five-story atrium extends out over the street with the intention of bringing those who might be reticent in. Panoramic views of St Paul's Cathedral are offered by the upper level café. Although the London Borough of Tower Hamlets has had financial help for these projects from such sources as UK Online, the European Regional Development Fund, or the London Development Agency, funding is extremely tight and the architectural concept must take this fact into account while giving the public a new type of educational experience. As David Adjaye says with a laugh, "We aim to be the Robin Hood practice. For rich people we make things grittier, for poor people we make them glossier." While the Idea Stores show how he aims to bring quality architecture and a new life to libraries in an area of London that is not its richest, his widely published Dirty House, built for the artists Tim Noble and Sue Webster in Shoreditch, East London, provides an example of the other "gritty" half of his "Robin Hood" equation. "My architectural politics are the politics of inclusivity," he concludes. Funding for the Idea Stores has been raised by a variety of external regeneration organizations (such as UK Online, European Regional Development Fund, Single Regeneration Budget, London Development Agency), as well as by the London Borough of Tower Hamlets. Resources have therefore been highly constrained and the Council is required to provide a full account of what it spends on the projects.

Dieser Idea Store geriet größer als der in der Chrisp Street, ist jedoch auf allen vier Seiten mit der gleichen Glasfassade „mit einem sich wiederholenden Raster aus Platten aus farbigem und klarem Glas sowie aus glasbeschichtetem Aluminium" verkleidet. In der Absicht, noch zögernde Passanten anzulocken, ragt ein fünfgeschossiges Atrium über die Straße hinaus. Von dem im Obergeschoss untergebrachten Café bietet sich ein Panoramablick auf St Paul's Cathedral. Obgleich der Londoner Bezirk Tower Hamlets für diese Projekte finanzielle Unterstützung von UK Online, dem regionalen Entwicklungsfond der EU und der Londoner Development Agency erhielt, war der Etat äußerst knapp bemessen, und das Architekturkonzept musste dieser Tatsache Rechnung tragen, während es der Öffentlichkeit gleichwohl eine neuartige Lernerfahrung bietet. David Adjaye kommentiert das lachend mit der Feststellung: „Wir wollen nach Art von Robin Hood verfahren. Für reiche Leute machen wir die Dinge rauer, für arme Leute machen wir sie schillernder." Während die Idea Stores zeigen, wie er qualitätvolle

Architektur und neues Leben für die Bibliotheken in eines der weniger begüterten Viertel Londons bringen will, stellt sein berühmtes „Dirty House", das er für die Künstler Tim Noble und Sue Webster in Shoreditch im Osten von London errichtete, ein Beispiel für die andere, „raue" Hälfte seiner „Robin-Hood-Gleichung" dar. „Meine Interessenpolitik in Sachen Architektur ist eine Politik der Inklusivität", erklärt er. Zusätzlich zu den vom Londoner Bezirk Tower Hamlets aufgebrachten Mitteln wurde die Finanzierung der Idea Stores von einer Vielzahl externer Sanierungsfonds (wie UK Online, Europäischer Fond für regionale Entwicklung, Single Regeneration Budget, London Development Agency) übernommen. Die Mittel waren begrenzt, und der Gemeinderat ist verpflichtet, für sämtliche Ausgaben im Zusammenhang mit diesem Projekt Rechenschaft abzulegen.

De plus grandes dimensions que les installations de Chrisp Street, la nouvelle Idea Store de Whitechapel fait appel au même principe de mur rideau « à motif répétitif de vitrages de couleur, de vitrages transparent et de panneaux d'aluminium doublés de verre sur les quatre façades ». L'atrium de quatre niveaux de haut s'étend jusqu'à la rue pour attirer les passants encore réticents à pénétrer dans ce type d'équipement culturel. Le café du dernier étage offre une vue panoramique sur la cathédrale Saint-Paul. Bien que le Borough de Tower Hamlet ait reçu des aides financières de sources comme UK Online, le Fonds européen de développement régional ou la London Development Agency, le budget était extrêmement serré, ce que le concept architectural a dû prendre en compte tout en offrant toujours une nouvelle approche de la connaissance. Comme le dit David Adjaye en riant : « Nous voulons être l'agence Robin des Bois. Pour les riches nous faisons des choses plus grinçantes, pour les pauvres nous les faisons plus brillantes. » Si l'Idea Store de Whitechapel montre comment il se propose d'apporter la qualité architecturale et de donner une vie nouvelle au concept de bibliothèque à une zone de Londres qui n'est pas parmi les plus riches, sa Dirty House, construite pour les artistes Tim Noble et Sue Webster à Shoreditch dans l'East London, illustre l'aspect « grinçant » de l'équation Robin des Bois. « Ma politique architecturale est une politique d'inclusion », conclut-il. Le financement des Idea Stores, en dehors de celui assuré par le London Borough of Tower Hamlets, est venu de divers concours extérieurs spécialisés dans les opérations de rénovation comme UK Online, le Fonds européen de développement régional, le Single Regeneration Budget, la London Devlopment Agency. Les ressources étaient comptées et le Conseil d'administration était soumis à un contrôle très strict des dépenses.

The Whitechapel Idea Store, with its higher profile, may bring to mind a small, attractive office building more than a library. Plans and an image (above) show the same curving bookshelves used in the Chrisp Street Idea Store.

Der gößere Idea Store in Whitechapel erinnert eher an ein kleines, attraktives Bürogebäude als an eine Bibliothek. Grundrisse und ein Foto (oben) lassen die gleichen gebogenen Regale erkennen, die auch im Idea Store in der Chrisp Street Verwendung fanden.

L'Idea Store de Whitechapel, de profil plus élancé, évoque plus un joli petit immeuble bureaux qu'une bibliothèque. Les plans et l'image ci-dessus montrent les rayonnages de livres sinueux déjà utilisés dans l'Idea Store de Chrisp Street.

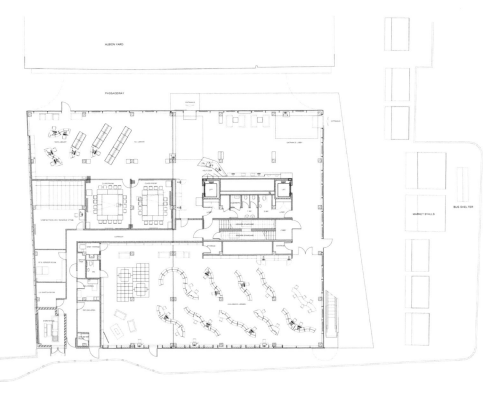

WILL ALSOP

ALSOP ARCHITECTS
Bishop's Wharf
39–49 Parkgate Road
London SW11 4NP

Tel: +44 20 79 78 78 78
Fax: +44 20 79 78 78 79
e-mail: info@alsoparchitects.com
Web: www.alsoparchitects.com

Alsop Architects is an architectural, urban-planning and multimedia practice based in London, with offices in Toronto, Singapore, and Shanghai. The studio is led by Professor William Alsop with a team of approximately 70 persons, including "architects, urban planners, multimedia artists, modelers, graphic designers, filmmakers, and fine artists." Born in 1947, **WILL ALSOP** worked in the office of Cedric Price (1973–77) and has maintained an active interest in art. Aside from his work in architecture, he has been a tutor of sculpture at Central St Martins College of Art & Design, London. Beginning in 1989, he worked with Jan Störmer from Berlin. Alsop's experience in "regeneration" projects includes the Regional Government Head-quarters in Marseilles; The Cardiff Bay Visitors' Centre; North Greenwich Tube Station; Peckham Library (named "Building of the Year" as winner of the RIBA's Stirling Prize 2000); and the Colorium Tower on the Düsseldorf waterfront. They have recently become involved in urban design projects in Barnsley, Bradford, Halifax, Stoke-on-Trent, Middlesborough, and Walsall. In London, recent work includes a medical school for Queen Mary College in Whitechapel and a new building for Goldsmiths College in South London published here. In the Netherlands, Alsop recently completed an urban entertainment center for Almere, a new city in Flevoland whose master plan was drawn up by Rem Koolhaas/OMA. Alsop's unusual College of Art and Design in Toronto, completed in June 2004, received the RIBA Worldwide Projects Award (2004), and the office is presently working on the redevelopment of Clarke Quay in Singapore.

BEN PIMLOTT BUILDING GOLDSMITHS COLLEGE LONDON 2003-05

FLOOR AREA: 3600 m²
CLIENT: Goldsmiths College,
University of London
COST: £10.2 million

Named after the former Warden of Goldsmiths College, University of London, Ben Pimlott, this 3600 m² facility includes visual arts studios, Goldsmiths Digital Studios and a research unit called the Centre for Cognition, Culture and Computation. The £10.2 million building (including a £3.7 million grant from the Higher Education Funding Council) is essentially a seven-story rectangular box 38 meters long, 15.5 meters wide and 26.6 meters high, erected on a 7.5 meter grid. 300 mm thick reinforced-concrete flat-slab floors supported on concrete columns provide the essential structure of the building. The top four floors of the building provide visual arts studio space with seminar rooms for the display and critique of the students' work. The studio spaces are lined in plywood and the floors covered with inexpensive chipboard panels that can be easily replaced or lifted to upgrade the building's IT system. Free-standing partitions divide the open studio floor to create student work areas. Upper-level studio space is 4.5 meters high. Three sides of the building are clad in silver-colored metal with punch windows, while the north elevation is completely glazed. Natural ventilation is used and, on the whole, an industrial vocabulary highlights a "tough" appearance. The concrete mass of the structure is exposed wherever possible, allowing the larger spaces to remain relatively cool. A two-story opening in one corner of the building is intended for outdoor work and display. The distinctive metal "structural scribble" that rises from this space has in a sense already become the symbol of Goldsmiths. Nine meters high, the 25-ton sculpture was made with a CAD model and 229 pieces of steel, of which 131 were assembled on site.

Diese nach Ben Pimlott, dem früheren Direktor des Goldsmiths College, University of London, benannte, 3600 m² große Einrichtung umfasst Studios für darstellende Kunst, Goldsmiths Digital Studios und eine Forschungseinheit „Centre for Cognition, Culture and Computation". Das Budget betrug 10,2 Millionen Pfund (einschließlich einer Zuwendung in Höhe von 3,7 Millionen Pfund vom Higher Education Funding Council). Es handelt sich bei diesem Gebäude im Grunde um einen siebengeschossigen, rechteckigen Kasten, der 38 m lang, 15,5 m breit und 26,6 m hoch ist und auf einem Raster von 7,5 m errichtet wurde. 300 mm starke, von Betonpfeilern gestützte Platten aus Stahlbeton bilden die wesentliche Konstruktion des Gebäudes. Die vier oberen Geschosse bieten Atelierräume für bildende Künstler und Seminarräume für die Präsentation und Diskussion der studentischen Arbeiten. Die Atelierräume sind mit Sperrholz verkleidet und mit einem Bodenbelag aus kostengünstigen Holzspanplatten ausgestattet, die sich leicht austauschen oder abheben lassen, um das IT-System des Gebäudes zu aktualisieren. Freistehende Raumteiler gliedern das offene Ateliergeschoss und schaffen Arbeitsbereiche für die Studenten. Die Höhe der Atelierräume im Obergeschoss beträgt 4,5 m. Der Bau ist auf drei Seiten mit silberfarbenem Metall verkleidet, in das die Fenster eingeschnitten sind; die Nordseite ist vollständig verglast. Auf Klimatisierung wurde zugunsten natürlicher Belüftung verzichtet, und insgesamt unterstreicht eine industrielle Formensprache das robuste Erscheinungsbild. Die Betonsubstanz des Gebäudes liegt so weit wie möglich frei, so dass die größeren Räume relativ kühl bleiben. Eine Ecke des Gebäudes ist über eine Höhe von zwei Geschossen ausgeschnitten und für Arbeiten im Freien und Präsentationen gedacht. Das aus dieser Ecke aufsteigende prägnante „Geschlängel" aus Metall ist in gewissem Sinn bereits zum Symbol von Goldsmiths geworden. Die 9 m hohe, 25 t schwere Skulptur entstand mithilfe eines CAD-Modells aus 229 Stahlteilen, von denen 131 vor Ort montiert wurden.

Portant le nom d'un ancien directeur de Goldsmiths College (University of London), cette construction de 3600 m² (budget : 10,2 millions de livres dont 3,7 de subventions du Higher Education Funding Council) accueille des ateliers d'art, les Goldsmiths Digital Studios et une unité de recherche, le Centre for Cognition, Culture and Computation. Il s'agit d'une boîte rectangulaire de 38 m de long, 15,5 de large et 26,6 de haut, élevée sur une trame de 7,5 m. Les sols en dalles de béton armé de 300 mm d'épaisseur et les colonnes en aluminium qui les soutiennent constituent l'essentiel de la structure. Les quatre niveaux supérieurs sont réservés aux ateliers et à des salles de séminaires pour la présentation et la critique des travaux des étudiants. Les ateliers sont lambrissés de panneaux de contreplaqué et les sols en panneaux d'aggloméré peuvent être facilement remplacés ou soulevés pour la maintenance des systèmes de communication. Des cloisonnements auto-porteurs divisent l'espace en zones de travail. L'atelier du dernier étage est d'une hauteur de 4,5 m. Trois façades sont habillées de métal argenté et de fenêtres à jalousies, et la façade nord entièrement vitrée. L'immeuble fait appel à la ventilation naturelle et, dans l'ensemble, à un vocabulaire esthétique « industriel » qui souligne son aspect « brut ». Le béton de la structure est laissé apparent à chaque fois que c'est possible, ce qui confère un aspect assez décontracté aux grands volumes. Une ouverture de deux niveaux de haut dans un angle du bâtiment facilite le travail en extérieur et la présentation de réalisations. Le « gribouillis structurel » en acier qui jaillit de la toiture est quasiment devenu le symbole de Goldsmiths. De 9 m de haut, cette sculpture de 25 tonnes a été dessinée par ordinateur et composée de 229 pièces d'acier dont 131 assemblées sur place.

The cladding of the building consists of floor-to-floor curtain-wall glazing for the north elevation and an aluminum roofing system formed from vertically ribbed panels that were stitched together on site for the south, east and west elevations.

Die Fassade des Gebäudes besteht an der Nordseite aus einer gläsernen Verkleidung, an den übrigen drei Seiten aus einem Aluminium-dachbelag aus vertikal gerippten Platten, die in situ miteinander verbunden wurden.

L'habillage du bâtiment consiste en murs-rideaux de verre sur la façade nord et en un système de couverture en panneaux d'aluminium nervurés assemblés sur place pour les façades sud, est et ouest.

Alsop's recognizable sculptural metal "scribble" was developed in "3D as part of an accurate CAD model from a series of repeated fabricated steel units. The units were then delivered to site and welded in location using a combination of accurate on site laser surveying and the original CAD model."

Alsops unverwechselbares plastisches „Metallgeschlängel" entstand „als exaktes 3D-CAD-Modell aus einer Serie gleichartiger, vorgefertigter Stahlelemente. Die Elemente wurden dann vor Ort angeliefert und mit Hilfe exakter Lasersteuerung und dem ursprünglichen CAD-Modell angeschweißt."

Le « gribouillis » sculptural métallique d'Alsop qui rend le bâtiment reconnaissable de loin. Il a été mis au point en « 3D sur une maquette détaillée en CAD obtenue par répétition d'éléments en acier. Ces éléments ont été livrés sur le chantier et assemblés par soudure au laser pilotée à partir de la maquette ».

FAWOOD CHILDREN'S CENTRE
LONDON
2004

FLOOR AREA: 1220 m²
CLIENT: Stonebridge Housing Action Trust
COST: £2.3 million

Setting aside some of the reticence that has characterized recent architecture, Will Alsop's goal is to "make life better through architecture." His Fawood Children's Centre is an interesting example of a low-budget (£2.3 million) structure based on simple ideas but carried out with brio. The brief called for "a nursery for 3–5 year olds: nursery facilities for autistic and special needs children, and a children's center with adult learning services—a base for community education workers and consultation services," all under one roof. Making use of prefabricated shipping containers and a Mongolian yurt, with external spaces protected by a partly translucent polycarbonate and steel lightweight roof, the center has tensioned mesh walls that avoid the problem of graffiti. Colored elliptical acrylic 'lozenges' give a bright and cheerful aspect to the mesh walls. The architect has generated a joyful space truly intended for small children that was easily and rapidly built, in the form of a single three-story enclosure. Alsop noted that outdoor play spaces in children's care centers are often underused because of the London climate, but, by sheltering even the external areas of the Fawood Centre, his scheme at least partially solves this problem. Alsop designed the play facilities in conjunction with a project artist who has specific experience in designing usable artwork and installations. Part of an overall plan for the use of the so-called Stonebridge estate being carried out by the Stonebridge Housing Action Trust, the Children's Centre is intended to be the focal point of a future park to be created after 2007, when nearby high-rise housing is scheduled for demolition. One challenge was to create a design that would be appropriate both for the present site circumstances and those promised for the future. Alsop is also due to build a Health and Community Building as part of the overall Stonebridge project.

Will Alsop zögert nicht, als sein Ziel „die Verbesserung des Lebens durch Architektur" anzugeben; die für die jüngste Architektur typische Zurückhaltung geht ihm ab. Sein Fawood Children's Centre ist ein interessantes Beispiel für ein mit kleinem Budget (2,3 Millionen Pfund) realisiertes Gebäude, das auf einfachen Ideen basiert, aber mit Elan ausgeführt ist. Die Ausschreibung verlangte „eine Tagesstätte für Drei- bis Fünfjährige: Einrichtungen für autistische und besonders förderungsbedürftige Kinder sowie ein Kinderzentrum mit angeschlossener Erwachsenenbildung – ein Standort für Sozialarbeit und Beratungsdienste", alles unter einem Dach. Das Zentrum besteht aus Frachtcontainern und einer mongolischen Jurte sowie Außenbereichen, die von einem teilweise lichtdurchlässigen Dach in Leichtbauweise aus Polycarbonat und Stahl geschützt werden. Die Wände bestehen aus gespanntem Drahtgeflecht aus Edelstahl, die dem Graffitiproblem vorbeugen. Dank bunter Ellipsen aus Acryl erhalten die Maschenwände einen bunten, fröhlichen Charakter. Der Architekt schuf eine kindgerechte, freundliche Umgebung; das dreigeschossige Gebäude konnte leicht und schnell errichtet werden. Alsop bemerkte, dass wegen des Londoner Wetters die Außen-

bereiche von Kindertagesstätten oft kaum zum Spielen genutzt werden. Indem er die Außenbereiche des Fawood Centre überdachte, löste er dieses Problem zumindest teilweise. Die Spielgeräte wurden in Zusammenarbeit mit einem Projektkünstler gestaltet, der über besondere Erfahrung im Entwerfen „benutzbarer" Kunstwerke und Installationen verfügte. Als Teil des Gesamtplans zur Nutzung des so genannten Stonebridge Estate, einem Projekt des Stonebridge Housing Action Trusts, wird das Children's Centre der Mittelpunkt einer künftigen Parkanlage sein, die nach 2007 entstehen soll, nachdem der Abriss der nahe gelegenen Hochhaussiedlung in Angriff genommen wurde. Die Herausforderung bestand darin, ein Projekt zu planen, das den gegenwärtigen Gegebenheiten auf dem Gelände ebenso gerecht wird wie den für die Zukunft konzipierten. Als Teil des gesamten Stonebridgeprojekts soll Alsop darüber hinaus noch ein Gesundheitszentrum und Bürgerhaus errichten.

Balayant les réticences qui caractérisent une certaine architecture récente, Will Alsop n'hésite pas à affirmer que son objectif est de « rendre la vie meilleure par l'architecture ». Ce centre pour enfants est un intéressant exemple de construction à budget réduit (2,3 millions de livres) reposant sur des idées simples mais brillamment mises en œuvre. Le cahier des charges prévoyait « un jardin d'enfants pour les 3–5 ans, des installations pour enfants autistes et handicapés et un centre pour l'enfance offrant des services de formation pour adultes, une base pour les travailleurs sociaux de la commune et des services de consultation... », le tout sous un même toit. Utilisant des conteneurs préfabriqués pour bateaux et une yourte mongolienne et se protégeant sous une légère couverture en acier et polycarbonate en partie translucide, le centre est enveloppé de parois en treillis métallique qui éliminent le problème des graffitis. Des losanges elliptiques en acrylique apportent une note de couleur vive et gaie. L'architecte a ainsi donné naissance à un joyeux espace sur trois niveaux vraiment adapté aux petits enfants qui a été aisément et rapidement construit. Alsop ayant noté que les espaces de jeux extérieurs prévus pour les enfants dans ce type de centre étaient souvent sous-utilisés du fait du climat londonien, il a prévu de profondes projections du toit vers l'avant pour remédier en partie à ce problème. Les espaces de jeux ont été conçus en collaboration avec un artiste familier de la conception d'œuvres d'art et d'installations « utilisables » par le public. Faisant partie d'un plan d'ensemble de mise en valeur du grand ensemble de Stonebridge par le Stonebridge Housing Action Trust, ce centre devrait devenir le point d'attraction d'un futur parc qui sera créé en 2007 lorsque les grands immeubles avoisinants auront été détruits. Un des enjeux de ce projet était d'ailleurs d'imaginer une solution adaptée à la fois au contexte actuel et à celui envisagé pour le futur. Alsop devrait également construire un bâtiment communautaire consacré à la santé dans une autre partie de ce projet de rénovation.

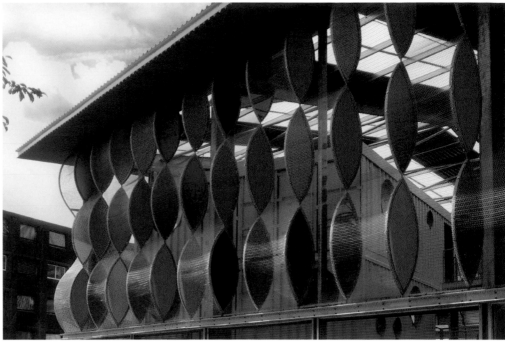

"Recycled prefabricated three-story sea containers, resembling giant children's building blocks," are is seen below inside the building, while the elliptical colored acrylic "lozenges" decorate the higher façades as seen above.

Im Gebäudeinneren sind „riesigen Bauklötzchen ähnelnde, wiederverwendete Schiffscontainer" zu sehen (unten), während oben die bunten Acrylellipsen abgebildet sind, die die oberen Fassadenflächen schmücken.

« Trois niveaux conteneurs de transport recyclés ressemblant à des pièces de jeu de construction pour enfants » s'aperçoivent ci-dessous. Des « losanges » elliptiques en acrylique de couleur décorent la partie supérieure des façades (ci-dessus).

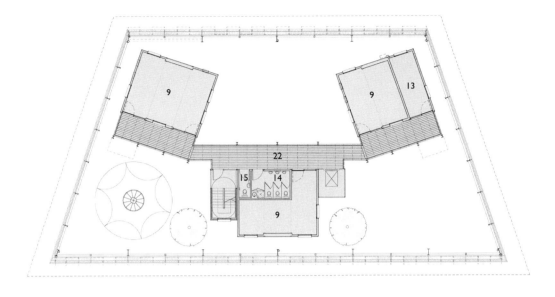

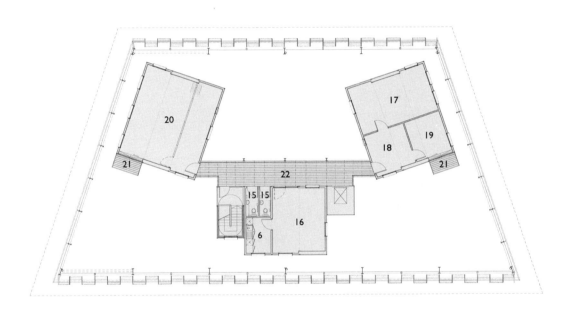

Floor plans for the center show the reception lobby (1), nursery spaces (9, 11), a cycle track (K), and a water garden (M). On the upper levels, further nursery accommodations (9) and the children's center (16–20) are visible.

Auf Grundrissen des Zentrums sind die Eingangslobby (1), Räumlichkeiten des Kindergartens (9, 11), eine Fahrradbahn (K) sowie ein Wassergarten (M) zu erkennen. Auf den oberen Ebenen liegen weitere Räume zur Kinderbetreuung (9) und das Kinderzentrum (16–20).

Les plans au sol montrent le hall de réception (1), les espaces de garderie (9, 11), une piste pour vélos (K), un jardin aquatique (M). Aux niveaux supérieurs, d'autres garderies (9) et le centre des enfants (16–20).

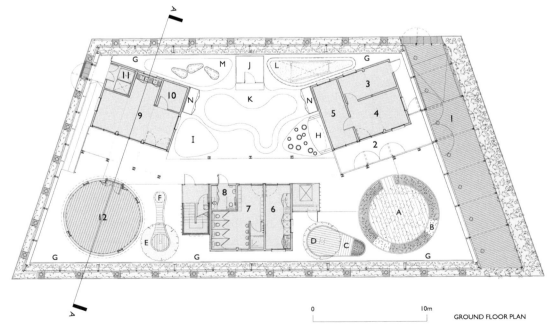

GROUND FLOOR PLAN

The bright, airy spaces inside the building are clearly well adapted to the presence of young children. The inventive use of shipping containers and brightly colored surfaces within the lightweight enclosure give it a unique atmosphere.

Die hellen, luftigen Räume im Gebäude-inneren werden von den Kindern offensicht-lich gut angenommen. Der innovative Ge-brauch von Schiffscontainern und leuchtend bunten Oberflächen im Inneren geben dem Gebäude eine einzigartige Atmosphäre.

Les volumes aériens et lumineux de l'intérieur du bâtiment sont à l'évidence bien adaptés aux jeunes enfants. L'utilisation inventive de conteneurs de transport maritime et de surfaces de couleurs vives à l'intérieur d'une structure aussi légère crée une atmosphère unique.

Partially visible in the images to the right, a "Mongolian Yurt provides supplementary indoor space, while adding richness, color and delight." As the architects conclude, "The design promotes complete integration of indoor and outdoor environments."

Teilweise sichtbar auf der Abbildung rechts ist eine „mongolische Jurte, die zusätzlichen Innenraum und überdies Vielfalt, Farbe und Spaß" bietet. Wie der Architekt abschließend bemerkt, „fördert der Entwurf die völlige Integration von Innen- und Außenraum".

En partie visible sur les images de droite, une « yourte mongolienne offre un espace intérieur fermé supplémentaire, tout en injectant davantage de richesse, de couleur et de plaisir ». L'architecte conclut : « Cette conception favorise l'intégration complète de l'environnement intérieur et de l'environnement extérieur. »

CARUSO ST JOHN

CARUSO ST JOHN ARCHITECTS
1 Coate Street
London E2 9AG

Tel: +44 20 76 13 31 61
Fax: +44 20 77 29 61 88
e-mail: info@carusostjohn.com
Web: www.carusostjohn.com

ADAM CARUSO was born in 1962 and studied architecture at McGill University in Montreal. PETER ST JOHN was born in 1959 and studied at the Bartlett and Architectural Association (AA) School of Architecture in London. Both worked for Florian Beigel and Arup Associates before creating their own firm, in 1990. They have taught at the University of North London, at the Academy of Architecture in Mendrisio, Switzerland, and at the Harvard University Graduate School of Design. Their recent and current work includes the Bethnal Green Museum of Childhood, Phase 2, London (2003–06); Brick House, London (2001–05); Centre for Contemporary Art, Nottingham (2004–08); the Gagosian Gallery, Britannia Street, London (published here 2001-04); a private gallery on Newport Street, London (2004–06); and a New Art Gallery and Public Square, Walsall (also featured here, 1995-2000). They designed the presentation of the exhibition of the work of the photographer Thomas Demand at the Palazzo Pitti in Florence, Fondation Cartier in Paris, and Kunsthaus Bregenz between 2001 and 2004 and the Turner and Venice show at Tate Britain (2003-04).

NEW ART GALLERY & PUBLIC SQUARE
WALSALL 1995 - 2000

FLOOR AREA: 5000 m² (excluding public square)
CLIENT: Walsall Metropolitan Borough Council
COST: £21 million

The New Art Gallery in Walsall was built to house the Garman Ryan Collection, donated by Kathleen Garman, widow of the sculptor Jacob Epstein. Financed in part by the Arts Council Lottery, ERDf, and City Challenge, the £21 million project is part of a regeneration scheme for the area east of the town. The actual client was the Walsall Metropolitan Borough Council. The 5000 m² facility contains temporary exhibition space, education facilities, a conference room, a bookshop, and restaurant as well as the permanent exhibition galleries. The architects proposed a tower clad in pale terracotta tiles, marking the head of a canal on the site that was previously used as an industrial wharf. As the architects say, revealing the rather conflicting goals of the design, "While the use of a clay cladding relates to the hard brick and terracotta common to all industrial and public buildings in the Midlands, the surface of the building is fragile and thin, wrapping and disguising the complexity of the interior like the feathers of a bird. The dispersed pattern of flush windows and individual overlapping tiles is intended to give the building a surface of fine decoration such as is found in the lasting architecture of Victorian civic building." In choosing the tower form because of its symbolic presence, but also to allow for small exhibition floors, the architects have taken into account the small scale of most of the works in the collection. The artists Richard Wentworth and Catherine Yass designed the public square around the building.

Die New Art Gallery in Walsall wurde erbaut, um die Garman Ryan Collection aufzunehmen, eine Schenkung von Kathleen Garman, der Witwe des Bildhauers Jacob Epstein. Das zum Teil von der Arts Council Lottery, ERDF und City Challenge finanzierte, 21 Millionen Pfund teure Projekt ist Teil eines Sanierungsplans für den im Osten der Stadt gelegenen Bezirk. Der eigentliche Auftraggeber ist der Walsall Metropolitan Borough Council. Der 5000 m² große Komplex umfasst Raum für Wechselausstellungen, Bildungseinrichtungen, einen Konferenzraum, einen Buchladen und ein Restaurant sowie Galerieräume für die Museumsbestände. Die Architekten planten einen mit hellen Terrakottaplatten verkleideten Turm, der das obere Ende eines Kanals auf dem früher als Industriehafen genutzten Gelände markiert. In den Äußerungen der Architekten offenbaren sich die recht gegensätzlichen Ziele des Entwurfs: „Während die Verkleidung mit Ton Bezug nimmt auf gebrannte Ziegel und Terrakotta, die für sämtliche industriellen und öffentlichen Bauten in den Midlands typischen Materialien, ist die Oberfläche des Gebäudes zerbrechlich und dünn; wie das Federkleid eines Vogels umhüllt und versteckt sie die Komplexität des Innenraums. Das unregelmäßige Raster aus bündig eingesetzten Fenstern und einzelnen, sich überlappenden Platten soll dem Bau eine dekorative Fassade verleihen, wie man sie in der Architektur städtischer Bauten aus viktorianischer Zeit findet." Die Architekten wählten die Turmform – zum einen wegen deren Symbolik, zum anderen, um kleine Ausstellungsflächen zur Verfügung zu stellen, wobei sie die Tatsache berücksichtigten, dass es sich bei einem Großteil der Sammlungsstücke um kleine Formate handelt. Der Platz, der das Gebäude umgibt, wurde von den Künstlern Richard Wentworth und Catherine Yass gestaltet.

Cette nouvelle galerie d'art a été édifiée pour recevoir la collection Garman Ryan, une donation de Kathleen Garman, veuve du sculpteur Jacob Epstein. Financée en partie par l'Arts Council Lottery, ERDF et City Challenge, ce projet d'une valeur de 21 millions de livres fait partie du programme de réhabilitation d'un quartier défavorisé. Le maître d'ouvrage est le Walsall Metropolitan Borough Council. Le bâtiment de 5000 m² abrite des expositions temporaires, des installations pour l'enseignement, une salle de conférences, une librairie, un restaurant ainsi que les galeries d'exposition permanente. Les architectes ont proposé une tour habillée de terre cuite de couleur pâle marquant le débouché d'un canal sur le site qui était un ancien appontement industriel. L'architecte a expliqué lui-même les objectifs assez conflictuels du projet : « Si le recours à un habillage de terre cuite renvoie à la brique et à la terre cuite présentes dans tous les bâtiments publics et industriels des Midlands, la surface du bâtiment reste d'aspect fragile, sans épaisseur, enveloppant et masquant la complexité de l'intérieur à la manière de plumes d'oiseau. La répartition dispersée des fenêtres à fleur de façade et le recouvrement des carreaux créent une surface décorative raffinée du type de celle que l'on trouve dans certains témoignages durables de l'architecture civile victorienne. » La forme de la tour a été retenue pour sa forte présence symbolique, et génère des espaces d'exposition de surface limitée qui conviennent à la taille réduite de la plupart des œuvres de la collection. Les artistes Richard Wentworth et Catherine Yass ont conçu la place publique aménagée autour du bâtiment.

The architects refer to the "austere and tough architecture of the warehouses and factories beside the side and visible to the horizon" to describe this tower located at the head of a canal.

Zur Erläuterung des Erscheinungsbilds dieses Turms am oberen Ende eines Kanals verweisen die Architekten auf die „bis zum Horizont sichtbare nüchterne, robuste Architektur der Lagerhäuser und Fabriken".

Les architectes se réfèrent à « l'architecture austère et brutale des entrepôts et des usines non loin du site et visibles à l'horizon » pour expliquer l'aspect de cette tour située au début d'un canal.

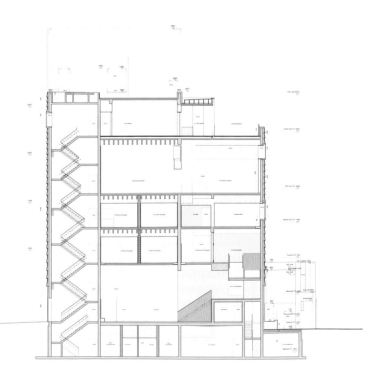
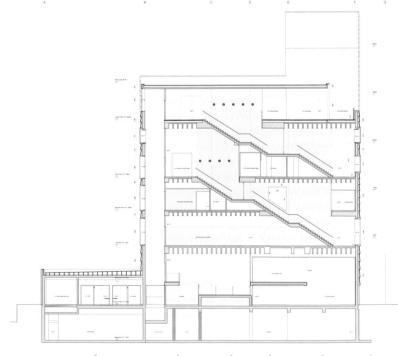

The exhibition areas are located around
a central hall on the first and second floors,
with an emphasis placed on a domestic scale
and windows that open over the town.
A combination of stairs and elevators encour-
ages a variety of different possible types of
movement through the space.

Die Ausstellungsflächen umgeben im ersten
und zweiten Geschoss eine zentrale Halle,
wobei großer Wert auf menschlichen Maßstab
und Fenster mit Ausblicken über die Stadt
gelegt wurde. Die Kombination von Treppen
und Aufzügen bietet viele Varianten, sich
durch die Räume zu bewegen.

Les zones d'exposition sont implantées autour
d'un hall central au rez-de-chaussée et au
premier étage, l'accent étant mis sur la conservation d'une échelle humaine et d'ouvertures
sur la ville. Une combinaison d'escaliers et
d'ascenseurs multiplie les possibilités de
déplacement dans les lieux.

GAGOSIAN GALLERY BRITANNIA STREET LONDON 2003-04

AREA: 1300 m²
CLIENT: Gagosian Gallery
COST: £2,4 million

The Gagosian Gallery, based in New York and Los Angeles, has been present in London for a number of years near Piccadilly. Their decision to renovate a 1400 m² former municipal garage near King's Cross Station and the British Library in London marks a shift away from some of the more traditional gallery areas in the capital. The ground-floor space is vast and high enough to accommodate major works by such artists as Richard Serra, like Gagosian's spaces in Chelsea (New York) or Beverly Hills (Los Angeles). As the architects say, "The most important issue in the design was to make simple and robust spaces that could accommodate the wide ranging practices of the gallery's artists. The interior had to feel solid and permanent, as well as provide a wide flexibility in how the different spaces could be interconnected and divided. Natural light levels of 650 lux had to be achieved on the walls in addition to a completely flexible artificial lighting installation." The main gallery space, 28 meters long, 13 meters wide, and 5.5 meters high, is a new structure that the architects placed in the center of the site, while another similarly shaped but slightly smaller space was inserted into an existing shed on the western edge of the site. White throughout, with a blasted concrete slab floor, the gallery space is austere but bright and obviously efficient. The vocabulary of the architects is tough but subtle, as would seem fully appropriate for the contemporary art that is exhibited there. They have woven renovated and improved spaces together with pre-existing façades or interior volumes into a coherent whole that meets rather strict functional requirements. The architects completed 400 m² of office space for the gallery in 2005.

Die in New York und Los Angeles ansässige Gagosian Gallery ist seit einigen Jahren in London in der Nähe des Piccadilly Circus vertreten. Die Entscheidung der Galerie, ein 1400 m² großes ehemaliges städtisches Parkhaus in der Nähe der U-Bahn-Station King's Cross und der British Library zu renovieren, markiert eine Bewegung weg von einigen der traditionellen Galeriestandorte der Hauptstadt. Der Raum im Erdgeschoss ist ausgedehnt und hoch genug, um bedeutenden Werken von Künstlern wie Richard Serra Platz zu bieten, ähnlich den Räumlichkeiten, über die Gagosian in Chelsea (New York) oder Beverly Hills (Los Angeles) verfügt. Nach den Worten der Architekten ging es beim Entwerfen „in der Hauptsache darum, schlichte, strapazierfähige Räume zu schaffen, die den weit gefächerten Techniken der hier vertretenen Künstler Platz bieten. Der Innenraum soll Solidität und Dauerhaftigkeit ausstrahlen und darüber hinaus größtmögliche Flexibilität bieten, was die Verbindung oder Abteilung von einzelnen Räumen anbelangt. An den Wänden soll eine Tageslichtkonzentration von 650 Lux erreichbar sein, zusätzlich zu einer völlig flexiblen Beleuchtungsanlage." Bei der 28 m langen, 13 m breiten und 5,5 m hohen Hauptgalerie handelt es sich um einen Neubau, den die Architekten in das Zentrum des Geländes stellten, während ein weiterer ähnlich gestalteter, etwas kleinerer Raum in ein vorhandenes Lagerhaus am Westrand des Geländes eingefügt wurde. Der zur Gänze weiß verputzte Galerieraum mit seinen sandgestrahlten Böden aus Betonplatten wirkt asketisch, hell und offenkundig funktionell. Die Formensprache der Architekten ist robust, aber subtil, was zu der dort ausgestellten zeitgenössischen Kunst sehr passend erscheint. Es ist den Architekten gelungen, renovierte und neu gestaltete Räume mit vorhandenen Fassaden oder Interieurs zu einem kohärenten Ganzen zu verbinden, das präzisen funktionalen Anforderungen gerecht wird. 2005 stellten die Architekten zusätzlich 400 m² Büroraum für die Galerie fertig.

Basée à New York et Los Angeles, la Gagosian Gallery était déjà présente depuis quelques années à Londres, à proximité de Piccadilly. Sa décision de rénover un ancien garage municipal de 1400 m² près de King's Cross et de la British Library marque une rupture par rapport aux quartiers des galeries traditionnelles de la capitale. L'espace du rez-de-chaussée est suffisamment vaste et haut pour recevoir des œuvres majeures d'artistes comme Richard Serra, de même que dans les galeries Gagosian de Chelsea (New York) ou de Beverly Hills (Los Angeles). Comme l'expliquent les architectes : « L'enjeu le plus important était de concevoir des volumes simples et robustes qui puissent accueillir les œuvres variées des artistes de la galerie. L'intérieur devait donner un sentiment de solidité et de permanence, tout en offrant la souplesse nécessaire par l'interconnexion et la répartition des divers espaces. Par ailleurs, il fallait pouvoir disposer d'un niveau d'éclairage naturel de 650 lux sur les murs, en complément d'une installation d'éclairage artificiel complètement modulable. » Le principal espace d'exposition – 28 x 13 x 5,5 m – est un bâtiment neuf au centre du terrain, tandis qu'un autre, de forme à peu près similaire mais légèrement plus petit, a été inséré dans un shed existant à la limite ouest de la parcelle. Tout blanc, doté d'un sol en béton décapé, cet espace austère et lumineux est visiblement efficace. Le vocabulaire puissant et subtil des architectes convient à l'art contemporain exposé. Les volumes rénovés et améliorés ont été imbriqués dans les façades ou les espaces existants en un tout cohérent qui répond à de strictes contraintes fonctionnelles. Les 400 m² de bureaux de la galerie seront achevés en 2005.

Despite the external appearance of the buildings, the architects have succeeded in creating powerful modern exhibition spaces within, with natural overhead lighting and concrete floors that allow the works of contemporary art to stand out.

Ungeachtet der äußeren Erscheinung der Bauten gelang den Architekten die Schaffung moderner Ausstellungsflächen im Inneren mit Tageslicht durch Oberlicht und Betonböden zur optimalen Präsentation von Werken der zeitgenössischen Kunst.

Malgré l'aspect extérieur de ces constructions, les architectes ont réussi à créer des espaces d'exposition moderne et pleins de force, bénéficiant d'un éclairage naturel zénithal et de sols en béton au grand bénéfice des œuvres d'art contemporain.

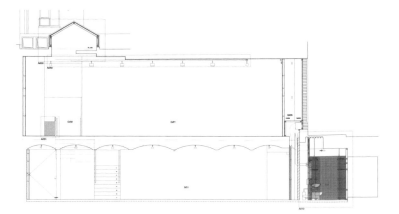

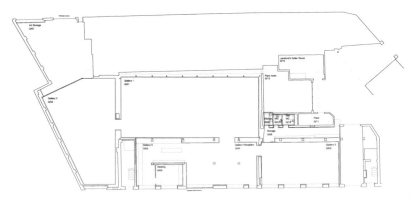

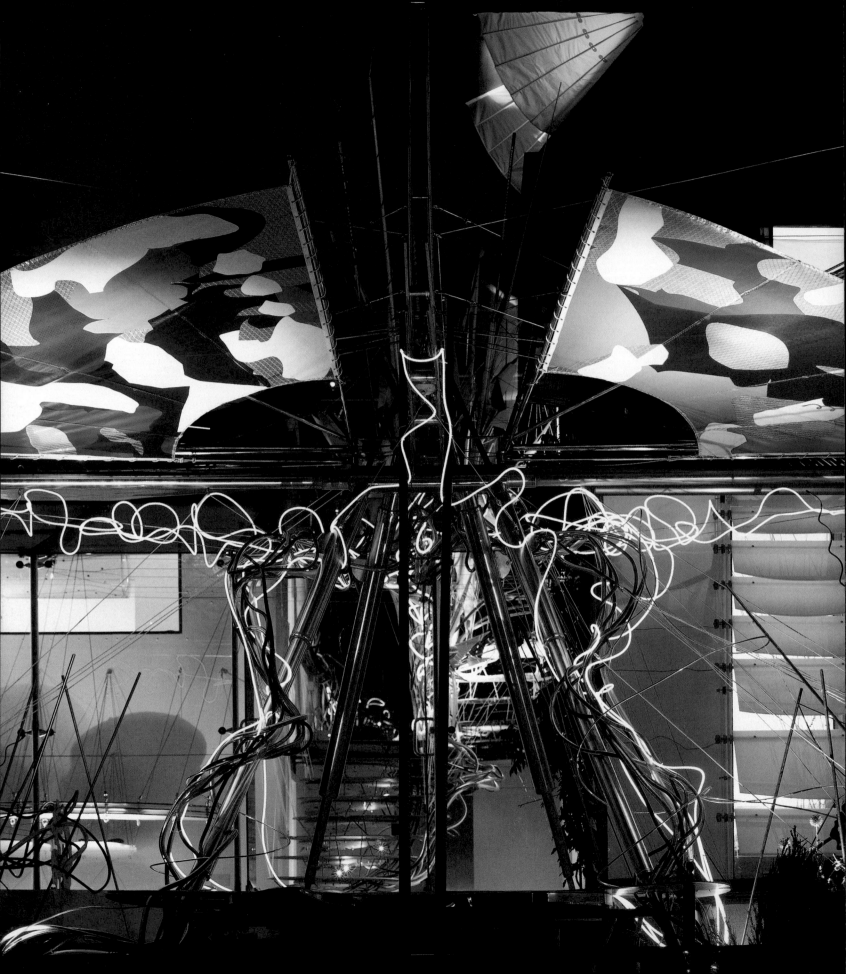

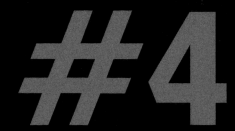

LAURIE CHETWOOD

CHETWOOD ASSOCIATES
12–13 Clerkenwell Green
London EC1R 0QJ

Tel: +44 20 74 90 24 00
Fax: +44 20 72 50 19 16
e-mail: laurie.chetwood
@chetwood-associates.com
Web: www.chetwood-associates.com

LAURIE CHETWOOD was born in 1957 and attended the Brighton School of Architecture, from which he graduated in 1983. He founded Chetwood Associates in 1992. The firm, which won the prestigious Architectural Practice of the Year Award given by *Building* magazine in 2000, currently employs 100 architects and has offices in London, Birmingham, and Leeds. Chetwood Associates "now specializes in sustainable, mixed-use developments, including retail, residential, and distribution in the UK and Europe." The Butterfly House, published here, was shortlisted for the Building of the Year Award as well as the Manser Medal. The Zetter Hotel in Clerkenwell won both the Architecture and Innovation Awards at the European Hotel Design Awards. The Office Space design for Egg Bank won the BIAT Award for Technical Excellence and was highly commended at the BCO Awards. Some of the office's most significant projects include: Sainsbury's Millennium Store, Greenwich (1999); The Brewery, Romford (2001); Egg Bank Offices, Derby (2003); Zetter Restaurant & Rooms, London (2004); London Underground Station, Brixton, London (2004); New England Quarter, Brighton (in progress); Gazeley Eco-template, Bedford (2004); Urban Mixed-use development scheme, Horsham (2004); Town Center Regeneration, St Austell (in progress); and Housing Development, Southampton (2006).

BUTTERFLY HOUSE
SURREY
2000 - 03

FLOOR AREA: 225 m²
CLIENT: Laurie Chetwood
COST: £500 000

This unusual structure started its life as a small wood-frame house from Canada, exhibited at the Ideal Home Show in 1930 and rebuilt on its current site in Surrey in 1948. It was purchased by Laurie Chetwood in 1993, mostly because of its attractive site. Plants growing around the house, such as buddleia, lavender, or poppies, attracted large numbers of butterflies, a fact that inspired the architect to create a new house out of the old one, whose architecture would relate closely to the insects. Planning permission was granted in 2000, and construction work took three years. As the architect says, "The Butterfly House is an experiment in architectural sculpture ... part family house, part art installation. The experience—both inside and out—is a riot of color, light and form, all of which celebrate the butterfly, one of nature's most beautiful creatures." The walkway and area to the north of the house are intended to represent the early phase of a butterfly's life, calling on muted colors such as monochromatic galvanized steel. Within the house the butterfly symbolically emerges from its cocoon. Organic imagery for the stairs, such as handrails of entwined carbon fiber rod, and fiber-optic cables evoke the unfurling of new wings. Chetwood says, "The main living space, an open-plan lounge and kitchen area to the left, looks again to these wings and flight in its design." The garden outside the living room is conceived as a perfect butterfly habitat.

Dieser ungewöhnliche Bau begann sein Dasein als kleines Holzrahmenhaus aus Kanada, das 1930 auf der Ideal Home Show ausgestellt war und 1948 an seinem heutigen Standort in Surrey wieder aufgebaut wurde. Laurie Chetwood erwarb es 1993 vor allem wegen seiner reizvollen Lage. Die um das Haus herum wachsenden Pflanzen wie Buddleia, Lavendel oder Klatschmohn lockten Scharen von Schmetterlingen an, ein Umstand, der den Architekten dazu inspirierte, aus dem alten Haus ein neues zu schaffen, dessen Architektur engen Bezug auf die Insekten nehmen sollte. Die Baugenehmigung wurde 2000 erteilt und die Bauarbeiten nahmen drei Jahre in Anspruch. Nach Ansicht des Architekten stellt das „Butterfly House ein Experiment auf dem Gebiet der architektonischen Skulptur dar ... zum Teil Familienhaus, zum Teil Kunstinstallation. Sowohl im Innen- als auch im Außenraum bietet sich ein großartiges Erlebnis aus Farben, Licht und Form, das den Schmetterling, eines der schönsten Geschöpfe der Natur, feiert." Der Fußweg und das Areal nördlich des Hauses sollen das Anfangsstadium im Leben eines Schmetterlings darstellen und verwenden dazu gedämpfte Farben wie monochromen verzinkten Stahl. Im Inneren des Hauses schlüpft der Schmetterling gleichsam aus seinem Kokon. Organische Formen bei der Treppe wie ein Handlauf aus gedrehtem Kohlenfaserstab und Fiberoptikseilen erinnern an das Entfalten der neuen Flügel. Dazu meint Chetwood: „Der Hauptwohnraum, eine offene Lounge mit Küchenbereich zur Linken, bezieht sich in seiner Gestaltung ebenfalls auf die Flügel und den Flug." Der Garten draußen vor dem Wohnzimmer ist als perfektes Schmetterlingshabitat konzipiert.

Cette très étrange construction a débuté par une petite maison canadienne, à ossature de bois, exposée à l'Ideal Home Show de 1930 et remontée sur son terrain actuel en 1948. Laurie Chetwood l'a acquise en 1993, surtout pour l'intérêt du site. Les plantes poussant tout autour, comme les buddleia, les lavandes et les coquelicots qui attirent un grand nombre de papillons, donnèrent à l'architecte l'idée de créer une nouvelle maison à partir de l'ancienne, dont l'architecture serait en relation avec les insectes. Le permis de construire fut accordé en 2000 et les travaux ont duré trois ans. Comme l'explique Chetwood : « Cette maison-papillon est une expérience de sculpture architecturale ... elle est en partie maison familiale, en partie installation. L'expérience – aussi bien dedans que dehors – s'est transformée en un feu d'artifice de couleurs, de lumière et de formes qui célèbrent le papillon, une des plus belles créatures de la nature. » L'allée d'accès et la zone au nord de la maison, qui représentent les premières phases de la vie du papillon, font appel à des couleurs sourdes comme celle de l'acier galvanisé. À l'intérieur, le papillon émerge symboliquement de son cocon. L'imagerie organique des escaliers, comme les rampes en tiges de fibre de carbone et les câbles en fibre optique évoquent un déploiement d'ailes neuves. « Le séjour principal, le salon à plan ouvert et la zone de préparation des repas à gauche rappellent également la métaphore des ailes et du vol. » Le jardin se veut un habitat idéal pour les papillons.

Elaborate drawings and images of the house show that this is no minimalist design. The very complexity of the forms, in principle drawn from nature, sets the Butterfly House apart from most contemporary architecture. It is a truly personal work.

Detaillierte Zeichnungen und Bilder des Hauses belegen, dass es sich hier in keinster Weise um Minimalismus handelt. Gerade die Komplexität der von der Natur abgeschauten Formen hebt das Butterfly House von der zeitgenössischen Architektur ab. Es ist ein wahrhaft individuelles Werk.

Les dessins et images élaborés de la maison montrent qu'il ne s'agit en rien d'un projet minimaliste. La complexité même des formes, en principe tirées de la nature, place cette Butterfly House très à part dans le paysage de l'architecture contemporaine. C'est une œuvre authentiquement personnelle.

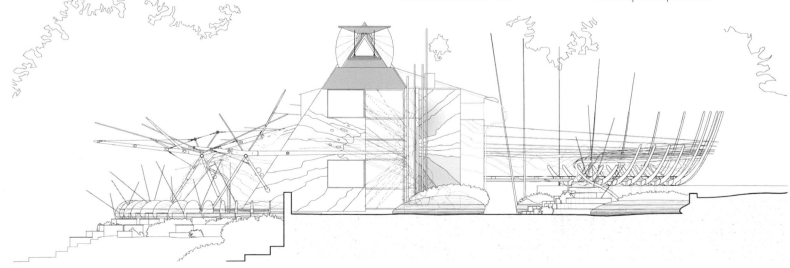

Wing-like structures evoke the butterflies that give the house its name. Despite the apparently eccentric nature of the architecture, it does fit into recent trends toward more actively decorative design, though here the intention is to refer to nature.

Flügelartige Strukturen evozieren die namensgebenden Schmetterlinge. Ungeachtet ihres exzentrischen Charakters fügt sich diese Architektur in den aktuellen Trend zu dekorativem Design ein, das sich hier allerdings auf die Natur bezieht.

Des structures en ailes évoquent les papillons qui ont donné son nom à la maison. L'aspect excentrique de l'architecture n'est pas étranger à certaines tendances récentes en faveur de conceptions plus décoratives, bien qu'ici la référence soit la nature.

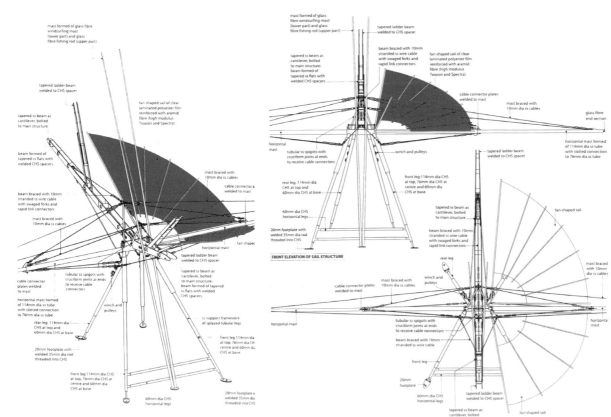

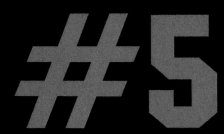

DAVID CHIPPERFIELD

DAVID CHIPPERFIELD ARCHITECTS
1A Cobham Mews, Agar Grove
London NW1 9SB

Tel: +44 20 72 67 94 22
Fax: +44 20 72 67 93 47
e-mail: info@davidchipperfield.co.uk
Web: www.davidchipperfield.co.uk

Born in London in 1953, **DAVID CHIPPERFIELD** obtained his Diploma in Architecture from the Architectural Association (AA) in London, (1977). He worked in the offices of Norman Foster and Richard Rogers, before establishing David Chipperfield Architects, London (1984). Built work includes: Arnolfini Arts Centre, Bristol (1987); Design Store, Kyoto (1989); Matsumoto Headquarters Building, Okayama, Japan (1990); Plant Gallery and Central Hall of the Natural History Museum, London (1993); Wagamama Restaurant, London (1996); and River & Rowing Museum, Henley-on-Thames (1996). His recent and current work includes: Landeszentralbank, Gera, Germany; Housing, Berlin Spandau; Office building, Düsseldorf; reconstruction of the Neues Museum, Berlin (2000–09); Ansaldo City of Cultures, Milan (2000–07); Figge Art Museum, Davenport, Iowa (2000–05); San Michele Cemetery, Venice, Italy (1998–2013); and the design of numerous Dolce & Gabbana shops beginning in 1999.

GORMLEY STUDIO
LONDON 2001-03

FLOOR AREA: 1000 m²
CLIENT: Antony Gormley
COST: not disclosed

This workshop and studio of one of England's best-known sculptors, Antony Gormley, is located north of the King's Cross railroad station in London, in a predominantly industrial area. The artist required space that was at once big enough to accommodate his largest works and yet retained a certain intimacy. He had worked in a converted laundry building since 1988, but here he obtained three times more space. Gormley, winner of the 1994 Turner Prize, is known for his 20-meter-high weathering steel sculpture, *Angel of the North*, set on a hill near the A1 motorway at Gateshead. With 1000 m² of gross floor area, the structure "abstracts the large scale, industrial architectural vernacular of the surrounding buildings." Pitched roofs allowing for ample overhead natural light and galvanized steel stairways define the structure, where interior whiteness and minimal design seem above all to form an appropriate, evenly lit environment in which the artist's creative process can develop without distraction. The building provides for an ample yard large enough for truck deliveries and is in general designed to scale of the heavy materials used by the sculptor. Functionally and aesthetically, the Gormley Studio is an exemplary instance of effective collaboration between an architect and an artist. The artist sought space that was particularly suited to his needs, but he also expected the architect to transcend the utilitarian, a hope fully met by David Chipperfield.

Diese Werkstatt mit Atelier für Antony Gormley, einen der bekanntesten Bildhauer Großbritanniens, liegt nördlich vom Bahnhof King's Cross in London in einer von Industrie geprägten Gegend. Der Künstler benötigte Räumlichkeiten, die einerseits großzügig genug sind, um seine zum Teil sehr großformatigen Werke unterzubringen, und die andererseits eine gewisse Intimität bewahren. Er hatte seit 1988 in einer umgenutzten Wäscherei gearbeitet, in seinem neuen Domizil verfügt er nun über den dreifachen Platz. Gormley, der 1994 den Turner-Preis erhielt, ist bekannt für seine 20 m hohe Skulptur *Angel of the North* aus oxidiertem Stahl, die auf einem Hügel nahe der Autobahn A1 in Gateshead steht. Das Gebäude mit einer Bruttogeschossfläche von 1000 m² ist eine Abstraktion der „groß angelegten industriellen Formensprache der umgebenden Gebäude". Dächer, die von oben reichlich Tageslicht einfallen lassen, und Treppen aus verzinktem Stahl prägen das Äußere des Baus, während das vollständig weiß verputzte Innere mit seinem minimalistischen Design vor allem einen gleichmäßig beleuchteten Raum bietet, in dem sich der Künstler ungestört entfalten kann. Der großflächige Hof des Gebäudes hat ausreichend Platz für Lkw-Anlieferungen, und der Bau selbst entspricht maßstäblich den schwergewichtigen Projekten des Künstlers. In funktioneller und ästhetischer Hinsicht ist das Gormley Studio das geglückte Ergebnis der Zusammenarbeit zwischen einem Architekten und einem Künstler. Der Künstler suchte für seine Bedürfnisse geeignete Räumlichkeiten, erwartete vom Architekten aber auch, dass er über das rein Nützliche hinausginge, eine Hoffnung, die David Chipperfield zur Gänze erfüllte.

Cet atelier, construit pour l'un des plus célèbres sculpteurs britanniques, Antony Gormley, se trouve au nord de la gare de King's Cross dans un quartier essentiellement industriel. L'artiste avait besoin d'un lieu qui soit à la fois assez vaste pour ses œuvres les plus grandes et conserve une certaine intimité. Il travaillait auparavant depuis 1988 dans une ancienne blanchisserie trois fois plus petite. Gormley, titulaire du Turner Prize 1994, est connu pour sa sculpture en acier patiné de 20 m de haut, *Angel of the North*, installée sur une colline près de l'autoroute A1 à Gateshead. Avec ses 1000 m² de surface, cet atelier « est une stylisation du vernaculaire architectural industriel de grande échelle de son environnement bâti ». Les éléments les plus caractéristiques sont les toits en pignon qui permettent un généreux éclairage zénithal et les escaliers en acier galvanisé. L'intérieur minimaliste intégralement blanc semble offrir le cadre et l'éclairage uni appropriés dans lequel un processus de création peut se développer sans distraction. Le studio, à l'échelle des matériaux lourds utilisés par le sculpteur, dispose également d'une vaste cour pour les livraisons par camion. Fonctionnellement et esthétiquement, cet atelier est un exemple de collaboration effective entre un architecte et un artiste. L'artiste recherchait un espace adapté à ses besoins, mais attendait aussi de l'architecte de transcender cet aspect utilitaire. Il semble que David Chipperfield ait su répondre à cette attente.

Although they appear to be repetitive, Chipperfield's forms echo nearby industrial buildings and provide a rigorous minimalism in which Gormley's art can flourish. Two galvanized steel staircases offer a counterpoint to the zig-zag roofs of the Studio.

Die sich scheinbar wiederholenden Formen Chipperfields orientieren sich an der nahe gelegenen Industriearchitektur, die sich durch einen rigorosen Minimalismus auszeichnet, in dem Gormleys Kunst zur Geltung kommen kann. Zwei Treppen aus verzinktem Stahl stellen einen Kontrapunkt zur Zickzackform des Atelierdachs dar.

Bien qu'elle puissent sembler répétitives, les formes imaginées par Chipperfield font écho aux bâtiments industriels voisins et offrent un cadre minimaliste rigoureux dans lequel l'art de Gormley peut s'épanouir. Deux escaliers en acier galvanisé viennent en contrepoint aux toits en zigzag de l'atelier.

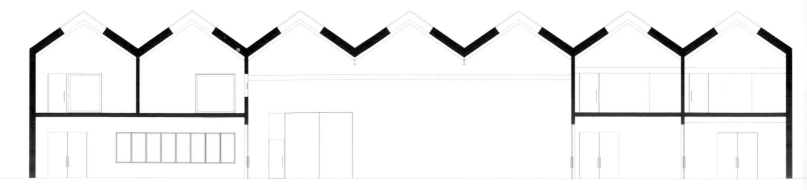

In both plan and in an image of the façade below, the Studio maintains a thorough-going rigor that nevertheless admits a certain number of asymmetrical gestures that give movement to the composition and serve the functionality of the building as well.

Im Grundriss sowie in der unten abgebildeten Ansicht der Fassade behält das Atelier die kompromisslose Strenge bei, die gleichwohl einige asymmetrische Elemente zulässt, die die Gestaltung auflockern und darüber hinaus der Funktionalität des Gebäudes dienen.

En plan et dans l'image de la façade ci-dessous, l'atelier conserve une rigueur affirmée. Un certain nombre de gestes asymétriques animent cependant la composition et participent au fonctionnalisme du bâtiment.

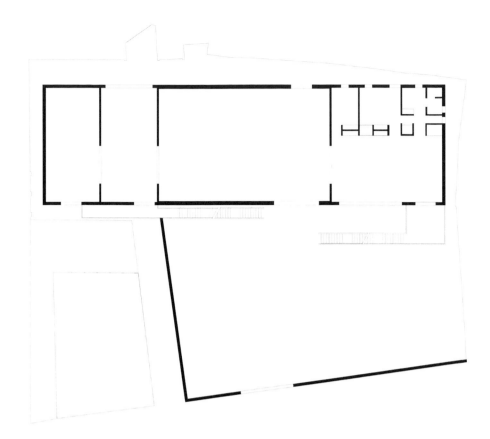

THE HEPWORTH WAKEFIELD 2003·08

FLOOR AREA: 5940 m²
CLIENT: Wakefield Metropolitan District Council
COST: £15 million

Wakefield in Yorkshire was the birthplace of the sculptor Barbara Hepworth in 1903. The Wakefield City Art Gallery, with its collection of works by Henry Moore, Ben Nicholson, Walter Sickert, Anthony Caro, Terry Frost, and Maggi Hambling, as well as earlier paintings, found its facilities in a Victorian townhouse inadequate and chose David Chipperfield to relocate and expand their facilities on the River Calder. The new facility will highlight a collection of thirty works in plaster by Hepworth, and the Wakefield Metropolitan District Council decided to name the 5940 m², £15 000 000 museum after her. Responding to the city's desire to improve its waterfront, the architect noted that: "The River setting and surrounding industrial character provides the context for the new Gallery. The former cloth and grain industries of Wakefield have left a number of finely scaled and positioned buildings along the water's edge. Our response to this urban setting reflects this built scale by organizing the building into a series of smaller components that could respond to different conditions around the new Gallery." The design is made up of twelve trapezoidal concrete blocks with sloped roofs intended to bring light into the gallery spaces along the river's edge.

Wakefield in Yorkshire war 1903 der Geburtsort der Bildhauerin Barbara Hepworth. Die Leitung der Wakefield City Art Gallery mit ihrer Sammlung von Werken Henry Moores, Ben Nicholsons, Walter Sickerts, Anthony Caros, Terry Frosts und Maggi Hamblings sowie älterer Gemälde empfand ihre Unterbringung in einem viktorianischen Bürgerhaus als unzureichend und beauftragte David Chipperfield mit dem Neubau und der Erweiterung ihrer Einrichtungen am River Calder. Mittelpunkt der Ausstellung im neuen Gebäude werden 30 Gipsarbeiten von Hepworth sein, und der Wakefield Metropolitan District Council beschloss, das 5940 m² umfassende Museum, für das 15 Millionen Pfund als Budget veranschlagt wurden, nach ihr zu benennen. Der Architekt entsprach dem Wunsch der Stadt, die Uferpartie zu verschönern, und bemerkt dazu: „Die Lage am Fluss und die industriell geprägte Umgebung bilden das Umfeld der neuen Galerie. Die ehemaligen Textilfabriken und Getreidemühlen hinterließen am Flussufer eine Reihe gut proportionierter, schön gelegener Gebäude. Wir reagierten auf dieses urbane Umfeld, indem wir diesen baulichen Maßstab aufnahmen. Wir teilten das Gebäude in eine Reihe kleinerer Kompartimente auf, die auf die unterschiedlichen Situationen um das Museum herum eingehen." Die Anlage besteht aus zwölf trapezförmigen Betonelementen mit geneigten Dächern, die für Licht in den Museumsräumen am Flussufer sorgen sollen.

C'est à Wakefield, dans le Yorkshire, qu'est née la sculptrice Barbara Hepworth en 1903. Logée dans une maison de ville victorienne peu commode, la Wakefield City Art Gallery qui possède une collection d'œuvres de Henry Moore, Ben Nicholson, Walter Sickert, Anthony Caro, Terry Frost et Maggi Hambling ainsi que des peintures plus anciennes, a fait appel à David Chipperfield pour édifier un bâtiment plus vaste au bord de la rivière Calder. Les nouvelles installations mettront en valeur une collection de trente plâtres de Hepworth et le Wakefield Metropolitan District Council a décidé de donner le nom de l'artiste à ce musée de 5940 m² dont le budget de construction s'élèvera à 15 millions de livres. Répondant au désir des autorités d'améliorer la zone des quais, l'architecte fait remarquer : « Le cadre du bord de la rivière et le caractère industriel du bâti environnant forment le contexte de cette nouvelle galerie. Le tissu et le grain industriels de Wakefield nous ont laissé un certain nombre de bâtiments d'échelle et d'implantation réussies le long des quais. Notre réponse à ce contexte urbain reflète cette échelle en organisant le bâtiment en une série de composants plus petits qui peuvent répondre aux différents états du contexte autour de la galerie. » Le plan se compose de douze blocs de béton trapézoïdaux à toits en pente qui génèrent un éclairage naturel intérieur abondant.

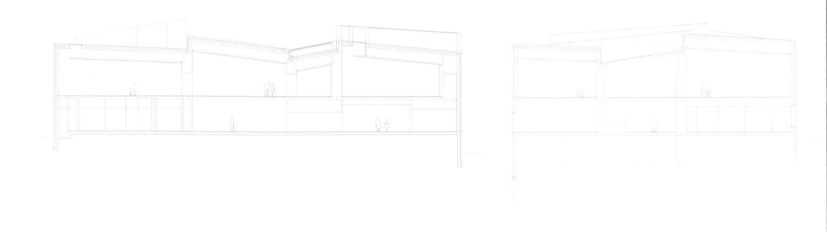

Plans, elevations and a virtual "model" of the project show the situation of The Hepworth in Wakefield. Although it is divided into a variety of different quadrilateral volumes, the result is anything but predictable.

Grundrisse, Aufrisse und ein virtuelles „Modell" erläutern die Lage von „The Hepworth" in Wakefield. Der Bau ist in eine Vielzahl verschiedener viereckiger Teile gegliedert und das Ergebnis steckt voller Überraschungen.

Les plans, les élévations et une « maquette » virtuelle du projet montrent la situation du « Hepworth » à Wakefield. La composition est divisée en une multiplicité de volumes rectangulaires de dimensions variées et le résultat ne manque pas de surprendre.

The Hepworth shows the architect's interest in basic geometric forms, but the way in which he has accumulated these forms creates a relatively irregular whole—building multiplicity from apparently rectilinear regularity.

„The Hepworth" dokumentiert das Interesse des Architekten an geometrischen Grundformen. Die Art, wie er diese Formen zusammensetzte, ließ jedoch ein eher unregelmäßiges Ganzes entstehen – bauliche Vielfalt aus scheinbar gradliniger Regelmäßigkeit.

« The Hepworth » illustre l'intérêt de l'architecte pour les formes géométriques de base, mais la façon dont il les accumule crée un ensemble relativement irrégulier. La multiplicité naît de la régularité rectiligne apparente.

6

EDWARD CULLINAN

EDWARD CULLINAN ARCHITECTS
1 Baldwin Terrace
London N1 7RU

Tel: +44 20 77 04 19 75
Fax: +44 20 73 54 27 39
e-mail: eca@ecarch.co.uk
Web: www.edwardcullinan
architects.com

Born in London in 1931, **EDWARD CULLINAN** was educated at Cambridge (1951–54), the Architectural Association (AA) in London, and Berkeley (1954–56). He worked for Denys Lasdun (1958–65), where he designed the student residences at the University of East Anglia, before setting up his own practice in 1959 and starting teaching at Cambridge in 1965. He established Edward Cullinan Architects as a co-operative in 1965. He was Bannister Fletcher Professor at the Bartlett (1978–79), Graham Willis Visiting Professor at Sheffield (1985–87), George Simpson Visiting Professor at Edinburgh (1987–90), and Visiting Professor at the Massachusetts Institute of Technology, Cambridge (1985). He is currently a visiting Professor at the University of Nottingham. The firm's projects include: Minster Lovell Mill, Oxfordshire (1969–72); Parish Church of St Mary, Barnes (1978–84); and Lambeth Community Care Centre (1979–84); and Royal Military College, International Headquarters (1985–90). Recent work includes: St Austell master plan (2002); Masshouse master plan, Birmingham (2002); Clink Street (2001), a proposed mixed-use development in Southwark, London; New Gateway to Petra, Jordan (2003); New Gateway Building, Royal Botanic Garden Edinburgh (2003); Cambridge University Botanic Garden (2001); and the Stonehenge Visitor Centre (2000), the winning scheme in an international competition.

DOWNLAND GRIDSHELL SINGLETON 2000-02

FLOOR AREA: 1200 m²
CLIENT: Weald & Downland Open Air Museum
COST: £1.5 million

The Weald and Downland Museum acts primarily to restore and rebuild traditional timber-framed buildings. The institution required two new spaces: a climate-controlled storage area for its collection of historic artifacts, and a large open space in which to conserve and repair the Museum's collection of buildings. The response they found was the Gridshell, "a three-domed oak lattice structure, which was a collaboration between Edward Cullinan Architects, Buro Happold Engineers and the Green Oak Carpentry Company." The two-story structure has a 500 m² lower level (the Artifacts Store) in a 10 x 50 m configuration, and 700 m² above, with a 10.5 meter maximum height on the upper level, which is used for timber framing. As the architects say, "This is a rural building for the 21st century." Sophisticated computer modeling techniques, as well as physical models were used to determine how the complex structure would be designed and erected. Untreated timber floors, ample natural light and use of thermal mass in the soil to control temperature show the architects' concern with sustainability. Six tons of oak was used in what is described as the "first all-timber gridshell in the world," with a doubly curved 48-meter-long roof. A special node connector was designed for the structure and subsequently patented. Another unusual aspect of the construction was the use of a flexible scaffold that was progressively reduced in height, lowering the grid into its final shape. Short-listed for England's Stirling Prize, the Downland Gridshell demonstrates the unusual innovative methods and capacities of its architects.

Die Hauptaufgabe des Weald and Downland Museum, eines Freilichtmuseums, besteht in der Restaurierung und Rekonstruktion traditioneller Holzfachwerkbauten. Das Institut benötigte zwei neue Räume: einen klimatisierten Lagerraum für seine Sammlung historischer Artefakte sowie einen großflächigen, offenen Raum für Konservierungs- und Restaurierungsarbeiten. Diese sind nun in der „Gridshell" untergebracht, einer dreifach überkuppelten Gitterkonstruktion aus Eichenholz, ein Gemeinschaftswerk von Edward Cullinan Architects, Buro Happold Engineers und der Green Oak Carpentry Company. Der zweigeschossige Bau verfügt über ein 500 m² umfassendes Untergeschoss von 10 x 50 m zur Lagerung der Artefakte und ein 700 m² großes Obergeschoss mit einer maximalen Deckenhöhe von 10,5 m, das zum Bau von Holzrahmen genutzt wird. Den Architekten zufolge handelt es sich hier um „ein ländliches Gebäude für das 21. Jahrhundert".

Um zu entscheiden, wie der komplexe Bau entworfen und realisiert werden könne, bediente man sich komplizierter Computerprogramme und realer Modelle. Unbehandelte Holzböden, viel Tageslicht und die Nutzung von thermischer Masse im Boden zur Regelung der Temperatur zeugen vom Interesse der Architekten an nachhaltigen Lösungen. Für die, wie es heißt, „erste Ganzholzrasterschale der Welt", eine doppelt gekrümmte, 48 m lange Überdachung, wurden 6 t Eichenholz verbaut. Für die Konstruktion wurde eine spezielle Knotenverbindung entwickelt und anschließend zum Patent angemeldet. Ein weiterer ungewöhnlicher Aspekt der Konstruktion besteht in der Verwendung eines flexiblen Gerüsts, dessen Höhe schrittweise reduziert wurde, während man das Raster auf seine endgültige Form absenkte. Die Downland Gridshell kam auf die Auswahlliste für den Stirling Prize; sie veranschaulicht die innovativen Methoden und Fähigkeiten der Architekten.

Le Weald and Downland Museum est une institution dédiée à la restauration et au remontage de constructions traditionnelles à ossature en bois. Il avait besoin d'un nouveau bâtiment de stockage climatisé pour ses objets historiques et d'un vaste volume ouvert où réparer et conserver sa collection d'ossatures. La réponse est le Gridshall, « structure en treillis de chêne à trois dômes, fruit d'une collaboration entre Edward Cullinan Architects, Buro Happold Engineers et la Green Oak Carpentry Company ». Il se compose d'un niveau inférieur de 500 m² (l'Artifacts Store) de 10 x 50 m, et d'un niveau supérieur de 700 m² de 10,5 m de haut au maximum pour les ossatures en bois. Comme le précise l'architecte : « Il s'agit d'un bâtiment rural pour le XXIe siècle. » Des techniques de modélisation informatique sophistiquées ainsi que des maquettes ont servi à établir les plans et la construction de cette structure complexe. Les sols en bois brut, un généreux éclairage naturel et l'utilisation de la masse thermique du sol pour contrôler la température montrent le souci de développement durable de l'architecte. Six tonnes de chêne ont permis d'ériger « la première coque à structure au monde en treillis tout en bois », à toiture à double courbe de 48 m de long. Une pièce de connexion spécifique a été dessinée et brevetée. Un autre aspect intéressant de ce projet est le recours à un échafaudage souple dont la hauteur a été progressivement réduite, jusqu'à la forme finale. Nominé pour le Stirling Prize britannique, le Downland Gridshell est une brillante démonstration des méthodes et des capacités novatrices de ses architectes.

The undulating form of the Gridshell and its layered design obviously make it fit into its natural setting more readily than a Modernist geometric form. Although it may not be typical of contemporary architecture in the UK, it is an indication of the variety and inventiveness to be found there.

Mit ihrer Wellenform und ihrer im wahrsten Sinne des Wortes vielschichtigen Konzeption passt die „Gridshell" viel besser in ihre natürliche Umgebung als etwa eine modernistische geometrische Form. Dieser Bau ist zwar nicht typisch für die zeitgenössische Architektur in Großbritannien, er steht aber für die Vielfalt und den Ideenreichtum in diesem Land.

La forme ondulée du « Downland Gridshell » et sa conception en strates lui a permis de s'adapter plus facilement à son cadre naturel qu'une forme géométrique moderniste n'aurait pu le faire. Bien qu'elle ne soit pas typique de l'architecture contemporaine britannique, cette réalisation donne une image de la variété et de l'inventivité de ce pays.

7

DECOI
ARCHITECTS

MARK GOULTHORPE
MIT
Room 10-461
77 Massachusetts Avenue
Cambridge MA 02139
USA

Tel: +1 617 452 3061
e-mail: mg_decoi@mit.edu

dECOi is a small architectural/design practice that looks to opening the boundaries of conventional practice by a fresh and exploratory approach to design. In 1991 **MARK GOULTHORPE** established the dECOi atelier to undertake a series of architectural competitions, often with a theoretical base. dECOi's work ranges from pure design and artwork through interior design to architecture and urbanism. Projects include: Bankside Paramorph (addition of a penthouse to the top of a tower, published here) South Bank, London (2002); Glapyros House, Paris (2001); Dietrich House, London (2000); Swiss Re Headquarters (technical/design studies for Foster & Partners, London, 1998); Missoni Showroom, Paris (1996); and the Chan (Origin) House, Kuala Lumpur (1995). Art and research works include: Excideuil Folly (Parametric 3D Spatial Glyphting, Excideuil, France, 2001); Aegis Hyposurface (Dynamically Reconfigurable Interactive Architectural Surface, Birmingham, 2000); and in 1993, "In the Shadow of Ledoux," (an "application/implication" exhibition, Le Magasin, Grenoble). Born in Kent, educated in Liverpool and Oregon, Mark Goulthorpe established dECOi in 1991 after having worked for four years in the office of Richard Meier in New York. He was a Unit Master Intermediate, Unit 2 at the Architectural Association (AA), London (1995-96); and is currently teaching Advanced Digital Design at MIT.

BANKSIDE PARAMORPH
LONDON 2003-04

FLOOR ARÉA: 320 m²
CLIENT: Private Client
COST: not disclosed

This project includes the remodeling of an existing 320-square-meter flat and, above all, the rooftop addition of a 130 square-meter-aluminum honeycomb structure. Taken from airline or space technology, the aluminum honeycomb skin has sufficient strength to replace traditional structural elements and the addition is to cost no more than an ordinary space (about £500 000 in this instance). With half the weight of "normal" construction, the new elements are to be delivered in six sections and bolted together on top of this apartment building located near the Tate Modern in the Southwark area of London. Working with the engineers Arup, dECOi feels that their method of parametric modeling and their ability, with the use of new materials, to "make the skin the structure" is nothing short of revolutionary. Shaped something like a seashell, the addition is described by architect Mark Goulthorpe as an "accelerating curve," and he is not surprised that the mathematically derived shape approaches some of those found in nature.

Das Projekt beinhaltet den Umbau einer 320 m² großen Wohnung und einen 130 m² umfassenden Dachausbau in aluminiumverkleideter Wabenbauweise. Die aus der Raumfahrt entlehnte Aluminiumaußenhaut verfügt über genügend Formfestigkeit, um traditionelle Konstruktionsmaterialien zu ersetzen, und die Kosten für den Dachausbau liegen mit 500 000 Pfund auch nicht höher als bei weniger ausgefallenen Methoden. Der halb so viel wie „normale" Konstruktionen wiegende Aluminiumkörper wurde in sechs Abschnitten geliefert und auf dem Dach des nahe der Tate Modern liegenden Wohnblocks zusammengeschraubt.

Die Architekten von dECOi, die bei diesem Projekt mit der Ingenieurfirma Arup zusammengearbeitet haben, sind davon überzeugt, dass ihre Methode des parametrischen Modellierens zusammen mit dem Einsatz neuer Materialien durchaus revolutionär ist. Der wie eine Muschel geformte Aufbau wird von dem Planer Mark Goulthorpe als eine „sich beschleunigende Kurve" beschrieben. Es habe ihn zudem nicht überrascht, dass die mathematisch entwickelte Form Ähnlichkeit mit Gebilden hat, die man in der Natur findet.

Ce projet porte sur le réaménagement d'un appartement de 320 m² non loin de la Tate Modern (Southwark, Londres) et surtout sur l'addition en toiture d'une structure en nid d'abeille d'aluminium de 130 m². Empruntée à la technologie spatiale ou aéronautique, la peau d'aluminium en nid d'abeille offre une résistance suffisante pour remplacer les éléments structurels traditionnels et cette extension ne devrait pas coûter au total plus cher qu'une construction classique (environ 500 000 livres sterling). Pesant moitié moins qu'une solution « normale », ces nouveaux éléments ont été livrés en six parties et boulonnés ensemble sur place. Collaborant ici avec les ingénieurs d'Arup, dECOi pense que cette méthode de modélisation paramétrique et le recours à des matériaux nouveaux pour « faire de la peau la structure » est quasiment révolutionnaire. Pour Mark Goulthorpe, il n'est pas étonnant que cette forme issue de calculs mathématiques se rapproche de celles de la nature. Pour lui, ce volume qui évoque un coquillage fait penser à « une courbe en accélération ».

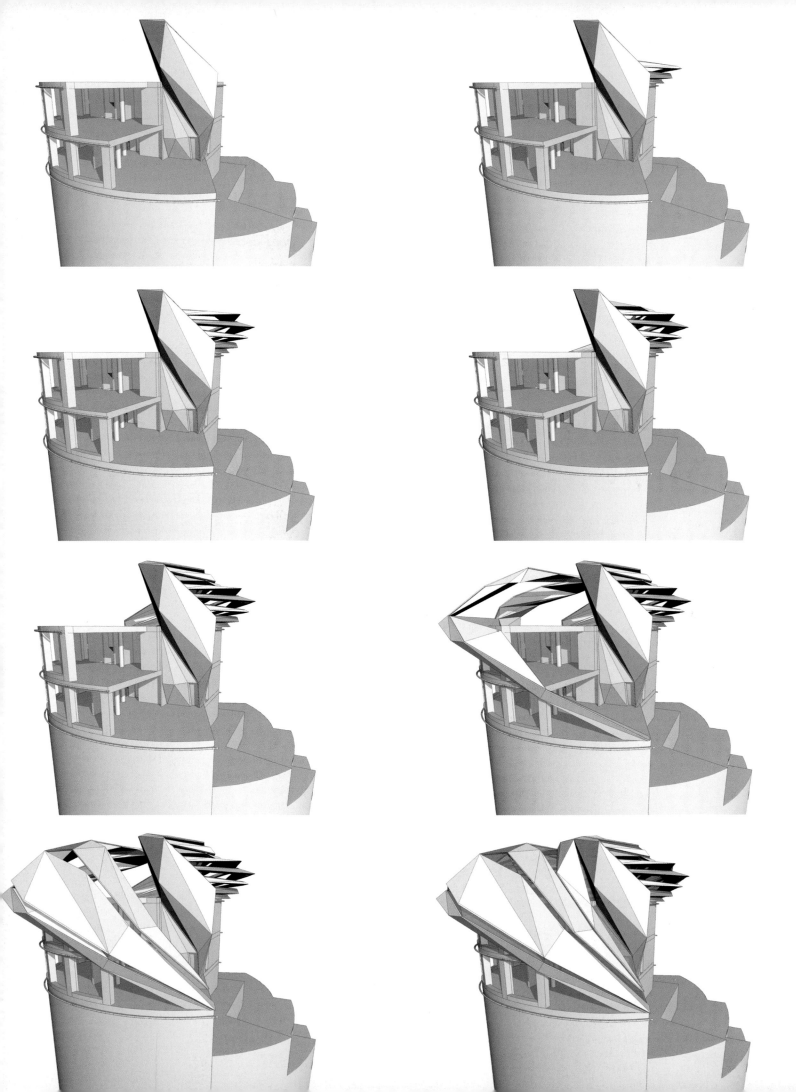

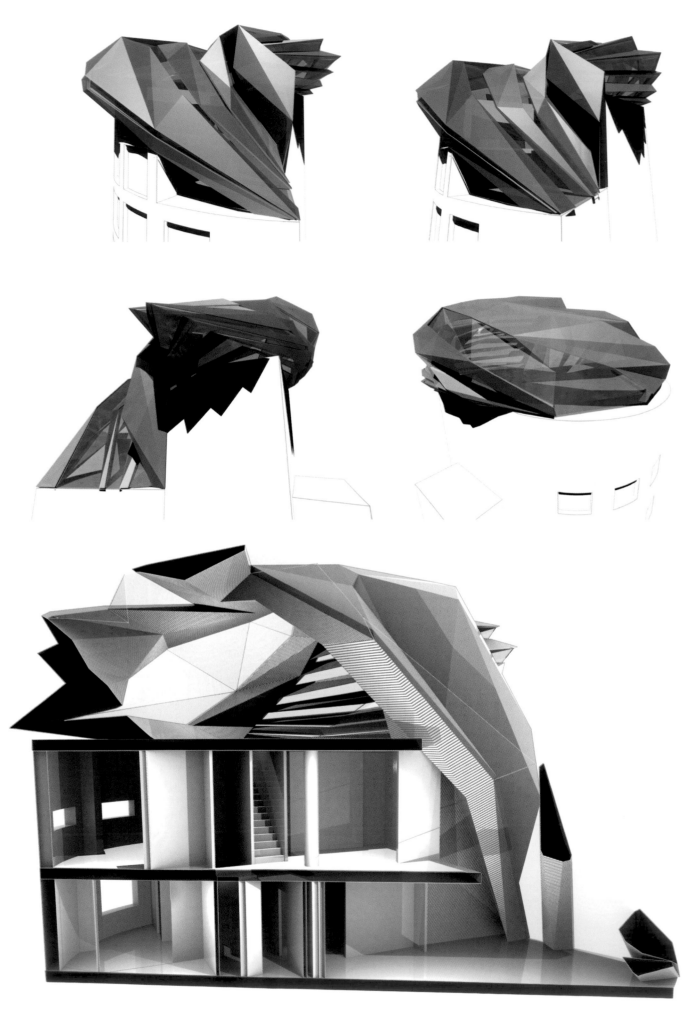

A computer generated image gives an idea of just what the Bankside Paramorph would look like in its real setting, right next to Tate Modern.

Eine computergenerierte Abbildung gibt einen Eindruck vom Bankside Paramorph in seiner realen Umgebung, in Nachbarschaft zur Tate Modern.

Cet image de synthèse donne une idée de l'aspect du Bankside Paramorph dans son cadre réel près de la Tate Modern.

An almost zoomorphic, wrapping design, the Paramorph demonstrates the new possibilities offered to architecture by sophisticated parametric modeling that can be used to command the manufacture of the unique parts of the structure without generating prohibitively high costs.

Mit seinem fast zoologisch anmutenden Design zeigt der Paramorph die neuen Möglichkeiten auf, die der Architektur durch ausgefeiltes parametrisches Modellieren beim Herstellen der Einzelteile mit nicht allzu kostenintensiver Struktur zur Verfügung stehen.

Projet d'enveloppe aux aspects zoomorphiques, le Paramorph illustre les nouvelles possibilités offertes à l'architecture par les techniques sophistiquées de modélisation paramétrique qui servent entre autres à passer commande de la fabrication de pièces uniques sans entraîner des coûts prohibitifs.

supported by

Audi

B.OPEN 13 JULY 200

8

ELLIS WILLIAMS

ELLIS WILLIAMS ARCHITECTS
Exmouth House
Pine Street
London EC1 0JH

Tel: +44 20 78 41 72 00
Fax: +44 20 78 33 38 50
e-mail: info@ewa.co.uk
Web: www.ewa.co.uk

Ellis Williams is an architectural practice with studios in London, Cheshire, and Berlin. There are three directors in the London studio, **DOMINIC WILLIAMS**, **TIM BAKER** and **BRIAN FAIRBROTHER**, all architects who have a wide range of experience in many different building typologies. The art team in London is led by **DOMINIC WILLIAMS**, who has a particular interest and experience in working on arts projects and directly with artists. Born in 1965, he worked at Skidmore, Owings and Merrill (1991–94) before joining the Ellis Williams Partnership in 1994. Past projects have included a virtual mausoleum, an experimental technology college and an art and music urban box thesis in Manchester, his hometown. He studied art at Manchester, architecture at Sheffield and "life on the road" as a guitarist with the band Junk. He recently completed the Zero IT retreat for Franciscan nuns in Derbyshire. Other work in progress includes the Didcot Art Centre (2006); Oriel Mostyn Gallery (2007); Wakefield Media College (2007); and the Longely Park Sixth Form College. The Baltic Centre was his first major completed work, the competition was won when he was 28 years old.

BALTIC CENTRE FOR CONTEMPORARY ARTS

GATESHEAD 1999 - 2002

FLOOR AREA: 8537 m²
CLIENT: Gateshead Metropolitan Borough Council
COST: £27 million

In 1994, the Gateshead Metropolitan Borough Council invited architects to submit ideas for the conversion of the Baltic Flour Mills into a contemporary art gallery. The objective was to "provide a national and international Centre for Contemporary visual arts." The existing building was 25 meters wide, 50 meters long, 40 meters high and originally contained 148 square concrete silos. These were removed in 1998–99 to create new space. The total internal floor area of the new gallery building is 8537 m² with spaces such as that on level one boasting a 7.4 meter ceiling height and a capacity to place point loads of six tons on the concrete floors—ideal conditions for often large or weighty contemporary artworks. Environmental concerns also motivated the architects who made provisions for high levels of insulation, efficient heat recovery, and air conditioning and ventilation systems. The building's thermal mass is used to limit summer temperatures and daylight is carefully controlled. As the architect Dominic Williams has stated, "The main aim is to allow contemporary art to happen in whatever form it takes. Often 'art' installations take on, or pervert, the nature of the space they occupy. The original function of the building was to collect, contain and distribute flour through the unseen workings of the silos. In many ways these activities would be unchanged, with the building now refocused to a new use. Works will come, be created, and travel on from the place, the function less secret though still housed between its sheer walls. Components such as the gallery floors, café and library, are inserted between these two walls to create a new living body within the building."

1994 lud der Gateshead Metropolitan Borough Council Architekten ein, Ideen für die Umgestaltung der Baltic Flour Mills, einer ehemaligen Getreidemühle, in eine zeitgenössische Kunstgalerie einzureichen. Angestrebt wurde „der Bau eines nationalen und internationalen Zentrums für zeitgenössische bildende und darstellende Kunst". Der bestehende Bau war 25 m breit, 50 m lang, 40 m hoch und enthielt ursprünglich 148 quadratische Betonsilos. Diese hatte man 1998/99 entfernt, um im Inneren des Gebäudes Platz zu schaffen. Die Nettobodenfläche des neuen Galeriegebäudes beläuft sich auf 8537 m². Dazu gehört u. a. der Raum auf der ersten Ebene, der über eine Deckenhöhe von 7,4 m sowie über einen Betonboden verfügt, der Punktlasten von 6 t tragen kann – ideale Bedingungen für die häufig großformatigen oder gewichtigen Werke zeitgenössischer Kunst. Für die Architekten waren darüber hinaus Fragen des Umweltschutzes von Bedeutung, sie sorgten für eine gute Gebäudeisolierung, wirksame Wärmerückgewinnung sowie Klima- und Belüftungssysteme. Die thermische Masse des Gebäudes wird dazu genutzt, die Temperaturen im Sommer zu begrenzen; Tageslicht wird kontrolliert eingelassen. Der Architekt Dominic Williams bemerkt: „Das Hauptziel ist es, der zeitgenössischen Kunst in welcher Form auch immer Raum zu geben. Häufig nehmen Kunstinstallationen den Charakter der Umgebung an, in der sie sich befinden, oder verfälschen ihn. Der ursprüngliche Zweck des Gebäudes bestand darin, in den Silos Mehl zu sammeln, zu lagern und es zu verteilen. In vieler Hinsicht bleiben diese Funktionen bestehen, obgleich das Gebäude jetzt auf eine neue Nutzung ausgerichtet ist. Kunstwerke werden eintreffen, werden aufbewahrt und von hier weitergegeben, wobei die Vorgänge weniger versteckt ablaufen werden als früher, wenngleich sie noch immer zwischen den steilen Wänden untergebracht sind. Elemente wie die Galerieräume, ein Café und eine Bibliothek wurden eingefügt, um im Gebäudeinneren ein neues, lebendiges Zentrum entstehen zu lassen."

C'est en 1994 que le Gateshead Metropolitan Borough Council a organisé un concours pour la reconversion des silos de farine des Baltic Flour Mills en galerie d'art contemporain. L'objectif était « de créer un centre d'arts visuels contemporains d'intérêt national et international ». La construction existante de 25 m de large, 50 de long et 40 de haut contenait à l'origine 148 silos de béton de section carrée, qui furent supprimés en 1998–99 pour laisser place aux nouveaux volumes. La surface utile intérieure de la nouvelle galerie est de 8537 m². Certaines salles mesurent plus de 7,4 m de haut et pouvant soutenir une charge de 6 tonnes/m², conditions idéales pour des œuvres contemporaines souvent volumineuses et très lourdes. Les préoccupations environnementales ont également motivé les architectes, qui ont abondamment utilisé l'isolation, la récupération de chaleur, la climatisation et la ventilation naturelles. La masse thermique du bâtiment limite la température intérieure en été, et la lumière naturelle est soigneusement contrôlée. Comme l'a écrit Dominic Williams : « L'objectif principal est de permettre à l'art contemporain de se produire, sous quelque forme que ce soit. Souvent, les installations artistiques prennent le dessus ou pervertissent la nature de l'espace qu'elles occupent. La fonction originale de ce bâtiment était la collecte, la conservation et la distribution de la farine par des processus invisibles de l'extérieur. À de nombreux égards ces activités seront identiques, le bâtiment étant simplement réorienté sur une autre fonction. Les œuvres arriveront, seront créées et voyageront d'un lieu à l'autre, la fonction, bien que moins secrète, restant toujours abritée derrière ces murs aveugles. Des éléments comme les sols des galeries, le café et la bibliothèque ont été insérés entre les murs pour faire naître un organisme vivant et nouveau à l'intérieur du bâtiment. »

Although the basic form of the Baltic Flour Mills has been maintained by Dominic Williams, large-scale elements devised in part with artists Richard Layzell and Jacqui Poncelet, added either on a temporary or permanent basis, signal the new artistic functions of the structure.

Obgleich Dominic Williams die grundlegende Form der Baltic Flour Mills beibehielt, künden zum Teil in Zusammenarbeit mit den Künstlern Richard Layzell und Jacqui Poncelet gestaltete großformatige Elemente, die zeitweise oder dauerhaft ergänzt wurden, von der neuen künstlerischen Funktion des Gebäudes.

Bien que la forme de base des Baltic Flour Mills ait été conservée par Dominic Williams, d'importants éléments permanents ou temporaires conçus en partie avec les artistes Richard Layzell et Jacqui Poncelet, signalent la nouvelle fonction du bâtiment.

Looking through the Gateshead Millennium
Bridge designed by Wilkinson Eyre Architects,
the Baltic marks a point at which culture has
come to take the place of industry, a rare
enough event to incite large numbers of
visitors to come and discover this new home
for contemporary art.

Beim Blick durch die von Wilkinson Eyre
Architects entworfene Gateshead Millennium
Bridge markieren die Baltic Flour Mills einen
Ort, an dem Kultur den Platz von Industrie
eingenommen hat, ein nicht eben häufiges
Ereignis, mit dem große Besucherzahlen
angelockt werden sollen, um diese
neue Heimstätte zeitgenössischer Kunst
zu entdecken.

Vu à travers l'arche du Pont du Millenium
de Gateshead (Wilkinson Eyre Architects),
le Baltic est un exemple d'activité culturelle
prenant la place d'une industrie, événement
assez rare pour inciter un grand nombre
de visiteurs à venir découvrir ce nouveau
foyer de l'art contemporain.

The interior forms of the former flour mills have been adapted in a surprisingly successful way to the exhibition of contemporary art, while maintaining a clear relationship to the original building, and its location.

Die Innengestaltung der früheren Mühle wurde in überraschend erfolgreicher Weise für die Ausstellung zeitgenössischer Kunst adaptiert. Dabei blieb ein klarer Bezug zum ursprünglichen Gebäude und dessen Umgebung erhalten.

Les volumes intérieurs des anciens silos ont été adaptés de manière étonnement réussie aux contraintes de l'exposition d'art contemporain, tout en conservant une relation claire à l'immeuble d'origine et à son site.

FOA

FOREIGN OFFICE ARCHITECTS
55 Curtain Road
London EC2A 3PT

Tel: +44 20 70 33 98 00
Fax: +44 20 70 33 98 01
e-mail: e-mail@f-o-a.net
Web: www.f-o-a.net

FOA is run by architects **FARSHID MOUSSAVI** and **ALEJANDRO ZAERA POLO**, and is "dedicated to the exploration of contemporary urban conditions, lifestyles and construction technologies." Aside from the Yokohama International Port Terminal, they have worked on: Barcelona South-East Coastal Park; Municipal Theater and Auditorium, Torrevieja, Spain; Publishing Headquarters, Paju, South Korea; Belgo restaurants in London, Bristol, and New York; and Blue Moon Housing and Tent projects in Groningen, the Netherlands. They have also designed a central police station (La Villajoyosa, Spain); harbor facilities for Amersfoort, the Netherlands; and a car park for Barcelona. They have recently been short-listed for the design of the new World Trade Center in New York and for the design of the new Centre Pompidou in Metz, France. Within the UK, they completed the award-winning design for Belgo Restaurant chain in Notting Hill Gate. Their most recent successful competition entry is the master plan design for the Lower Lee Valley and the London 2012 Olympics (featured here), which they did as part of a consortium headed by EDAW and HOK. Farshid Moussavi received her Masters in Architecture from the Harvard Graduate School of Design. She worked for the Renzo Piano Building Workshop in Genua in 1988 and for the Office for Metropolitan Architecture (OMA) in Rotterdam (Rem Koolhaas, 1991–93), and established Foreign Office Architects in 1992. Also educated at Harvard, Alejandro Zaera Polo worked with OMA in Rotterdam at the same time as Farshid Moussavi.

BBC MUSIC CENTRE
LONDON 2003-09

FLOOR AREA: 6500 m²
CLIENT: BBC/Land Securities Trillium
COST: £25 million

Foreign Office Architects won the competition for the BBC's new Music Centre against Future Systems, Ushida Findlay Architects and Zaha Hadid on November 17, 2003. To be called The Music Box, the building is planned to open in 2009 and will become home to the BBC Symphony Orchestra, the BBC Symphony Chorus, the BBC Concert Orchestra and the BBC Singers, bringing them together in one place for the first time. The Music Box is part of the new Media Village, the BBC's redevelopment of White City, and is related to the BBC's effort to open its doors to the local community in West London. Two studios for rehearsal, recording, and live performances with an audience capacity of up to 600 persons are part of the project, as well as support areas for rehearsal and practice. The White City site was developed for the 1908 Franco-English exhibition and was the venue for the 1908 Olympic Games. The Music Box will be at the center of a BBC campus with a daily population of 12 000 people. The broadcasting firm acquired the site in the mid-1980s and built an office building there in 1990. A master plan drawn up in 2000 for White City provides for up to nine new buildings, of which five are currently being completed. The construction cost of the Music Centre is estimated at £25 million. Its Studio 1 will be the base for the BBC Symphony Orchestra and its 105 permanent musicians, while the BBC Concert Orchestra and the BBC Singers will use Studio 2. Office accommodation for a staff of 40 is included in the brief. Community groups and schools will use the studios when the BBC is not occupying them, and musicians will be encouraged to give lessons to local residents.

Am 17. November 2003 konnte Foreign Office Architects den Wettbewerb für das neue Music Centre der BBC gegen die Konkurrenz von Future Systems, Ushida Findlay Architects und Zaha Hadid für sich entscheiden. Das Gebäude wird den Namen Music Box erhalten und soll 2009 eröffnet werden. Darin sollen das BBC Symphony Orchestra, der BBC Symphony Chorus, das BBC Concert Orchestra und die BBC Singers Platz finden, die damit erstmalig an einem Ort zusammen unter-gebracht sind. Die Music Box ist Teil des neuen Media Village, das Sanierungsprojekt der BBC für White City. Es steht im Zusammenhang mit den Bemühungen der BBC, ihre Tore der Einwohnerschaft von West London zu öffnen. Teil des Projekts sind zwei Studios für Proben, Aufnahmen und Konzerte mit einer Zuschauerkapazität von bis zu 600 Personen, außerdem Räumlichkeiten zum Proben und Üben. Die White City entstand für die französisch-englische Ausstellung des Jahres 1908 und

war im gleichen Jahr Austragungsort der Olympischen Spiele. Die Music Box wird sich im Zentrum des BBC Campus befinden und täglich von 12 000 Leuten besucht werden. Der Sender erwarb das Gelände Mitte der 1980er Jahre und errichtete dort 1990 ein Bürogebäude. Ein im Jahr 2000 erstellter Gesamtplan für White City sieht bis zu neun Neubauten vor, von denen fünf derzeit ihrer Vollendung ent-gegensehen. Die geschätzten Baukosten des Music Centre belaufen sich auf 25 Millionen Pfund. Im dortigen Studio 1 wird sich der Standort des BBC Symphony Orchestra und seiner 105 ständigen Musiker befinden, während das BBC Concert Orchestra und die BBC Singers Studio 2 nutzen werden. Teil der Ausschreibung ist außerdem die Schaffung von Büroraum für eine 40-köpfige Belegschaft. Falls die BBC die Räume nicht benötigen sollte, werden sie Gemeinden und Schulen zur Verfügung gestellt; die Musiker werden darin bestärkt, Anwohnern Musikunter-richt zu erteilen.

FOA a remporté le concours pour le nouveau Music Centre de la BBC face à Future Systems, Ushida Findlay Architects et Zaha Hadid le 17 novembre 2003. Appelé The Music Box (la boîte à musique), le nouvel immeuble qui doit ouvrir ses portes en 2009 abritera le BBC Symphony Orchestra et ses 105 musi-ciens permanents dans le Studio 1, le BBC Symphony Chorus, le BBC Concert Orchestra et les BBC Singers dans le Studio 2, tous réunis en un même lieu pour la première fois. Deux studios de répétition, d'enregistrement et de concerts en direct d'une capacité allant jusqu'à 600 personnes sont également prévus ainsi que les équipements techniques nécessaires pour les répétitions et la pratique musicales et des bureaux administratifs pour 40 personnes. Ces nouvelles installations font partie du Media Village, programme de rénovation de White City par la BBC. Elles manifestent les efforts de cette institution pour s'ouvrir aux habitants de l'ouest de Londres. Le site de White City est issu de l'exposition franco-anglaise de 1908 et des Jeux olympiques tenus la même année. La Music Box s'élèvera au centre de ce campus de la BBC qui accueillera chaque jour 12 000 personnes. La société a acquis cet ensemble immobilier au milieu des années 1980 et a déjà construit un immeuble de bureaux en 1990. Un plan directeur décidé en 2000 prévoit neuf nouveaux bâtiments, dont cinq en cours d'achèvement. Le coût de la construction du Centre est estimé à 25 millions de livres. Les associations et écoles locales pourront utiliser les studios lorsque la BBC ne les occupera pas et les musiciens seront incités à donner des leçons aux résidents.

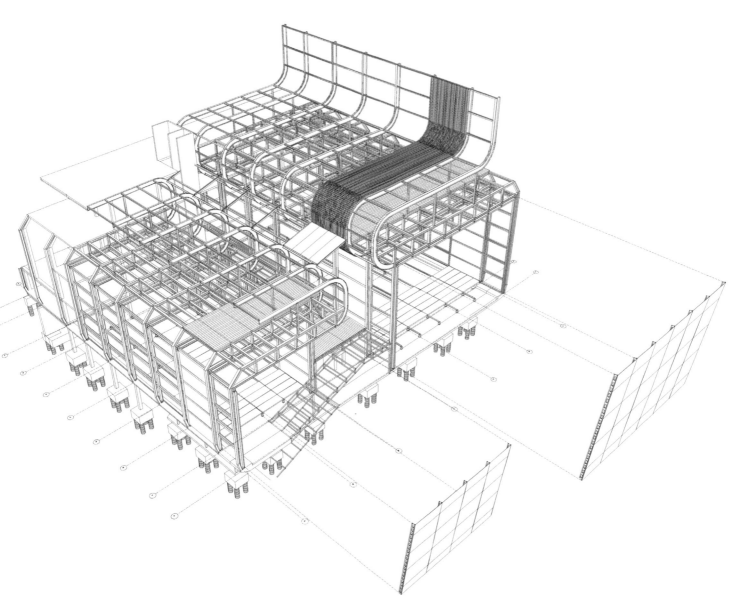

Perspectives and a drawing showing the building's structure reveal the continuous wrapping form of the design. Lifted off the ground a bit like a sculpture on its base, the building has large overhangs that provide covered outdoor space.

Perspektiven und Zeichnungen, die die Struktur des Gebäudes zeigen, lassen die durchgehende gewickelte Form des Entwurfs erkennen. Wie eine Skulptur auf ihrem Podest ist der Bau vom Boden abgehoben und verfügt über weite Überhänge, die Schutz bieten.

Les perspectives et un dessin de la structure illustrent le principe d'enveloppe continue. Soulevé du sol, un peu comme une sculpture sur un socle, le bâtiment présente d'importants porte-à-faux qui servent d'espaces couverts.

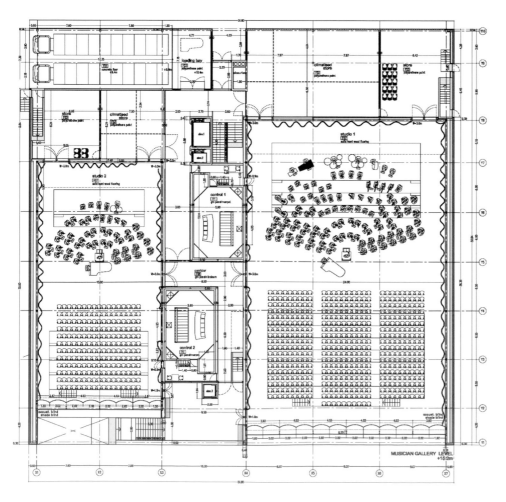

Plans, sections and perspective views show the bipartite arrangement with concert halls of two sizes. To the right, a foyer view gives an idea of the continuity of the architects' idea of wrapping surfaces, and a stairway links the two halls.

Grundrisse, Schnitte und perspektivische Ansichten zeigen die zweiteilige Anordnung mit den beiden Konzerthallen unterschiedlicher Größe. Rechts vermittelt der Blick in das Foyer einen Eindruck von der Kontinuität der umlaufenden Oberflächen. Das Treppenhaus fungiert als Bindeglied zwischen den Hallen.

Plans, coupes et perspectives montrent la disposition en deux parties et les salles de concert de deux dimensions. À droite, une vue du foyer donne une idée de la continuité des surfaces enveloppantes. L'escalier fait le lien entre les deux salles.

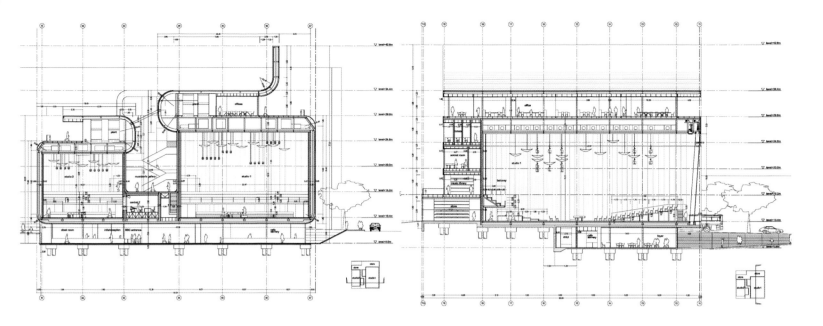

2012 OLYMPICS
LONDON
2004/2012

AREA: 215 ha
MASTERPLANNING CONSORTIUM TEAM:
EDAW, FOA, Allies & Morrison, HOK Sport
and Buro Happold.
CLIENT: London Development Agency
COST: £4 billion

As part of their efforts to obtain the 2012 Olympic Games, English authorities selected Foreign Office Architects (FOA) as designers for the stadium and the Olympic Park to be located in East London. As Alejandro Zaero Polo, chief designer on the project, explains: "We are trying to make the building communicate the idea of physical strength, sport, and movement. This is what constitutes the conceptual backbone of all the buildings. In the design of the Olympic Park itself, which is very different from any park that has preceded it, we are not creating another Olympic Village that is just a series of nice, white, modern buildings on a flat land. We are creating something that will grow out of the specific conditions and form of the Lea Valley, making it totally unique. This will be part of the lasting legacy for the local community." The regeneration of the Lower Lea Valley area is a major focus for the London 2012 bid, and it is already planned that The Olympic Village will be turned into housing with a newly built train line linking that community to central London in only seven minutes. The new 225-hectare Olympic Park will contain the Olympic Stadium, the Aquatics Center, a Velodrome and BMX Track, three sports halls, a Hockey Center, and the media facilities, each located no more than seven minutes from any other. The Park would also house the Olympic Village, accommodating up to 17 800 athletes and officials. The Village would be laid out to offer direct views of the Olympic Stadium. The designs for the proposed Olympic Park site are the result of 15 months' work involving hundreds of consultants, architects, designers, stadium experts, and the athletes themselves.

Als Teil ihrer Bemühungen, die Olympischen Spiele 2012 nach London zu holen, entschieden sich die Verantwortlichen in Großbritannien dafür, Foreign Office Architects (FOA) mit dem Entwurf des Stadions und des Olympischen Parks zu beauftragen, die in East London entstehen sollen. Alejandro Zaera Polo, der leitende Architekt des Projekts, erläutert: „Wir versuchen, mit dem Bau die Vorstellung von körperlicher Kraft, Sport und Bewegung zu vermitteln; sie bilden das konzeptuelle Rückgrat sämtlicher Gebäude. Mit dem Entwurf des eigentlichen Olympischen Parks, der sich von allen seinen Vorgängern sehr deutlich unterscheidet, schaffen wir kein weiteres Olympisches Dorf, das bloß aus einer Reihe hübscher, weißer, moderner Gebäude auf flachem Gelände besteht. Wir planen etwas, das sich aus den spezifischen Gegebenheiten und der Beschaffenheit des Lea Valley ergibt und dadurch ganz einzigartig sein wird. Es wird Teil des bleibenden Vermächtnisses für die örtliche Kommune sein." Die Erneuerung des Stadtgebiets von Lower Lea Valley ist Kernstück der Londoner Bewerbung um die Spiele 2012, und es ist geplant, das Olympische Dorf später in ein Wohngebiet umzugestalten, von dem aus man mittels einer neuen Bahnlinie in nur sieben Minuten das Zentrum von London erreichen kann. Der neue, 225 ha große Olympische Park wird das Olympische Stadion, das Aquatics Center, ein Velodrom und eine BMX-Bahn, drei Sporthallen, ein Hockeyzentrum sowie die Einrichtungen für die Medien umfassen, die sämtlich maximal sieben Minuten voneinander entfernt liegen. In dem Park soll darüber hinaus das Olympische Dorf untergebracht sein, das für bis zu 17 800 Sportler und Funktionäre ausgelegt ist. Direkte Blickachsen sollen es mit dem Olympiastadion verbinden. Die Entwürfe für das geplante Olympische Dorf stellen das Ergebnis von 15 Monaten Arbeit dar, an der Hunderte von Beratern, Architekten, Designern, Stadionexperten sowie Sportler beteiligt waren.

Dans le cadre de leur campagne pour obtenir les Jeux olympiques de 2012, les autorités britanniques ont sélectionné FOA pour concevoir le stade et le parc olympique situés dans l'est de Londres. Comme l'explique Alejandro Zaero Polo, concepteur en charge de ce programme : « Nous faisons en sorte que cette construction communique l'idée de force physique, de sport et de mouvement. C'est l'épine dorsale conceptuelle de ce projet. Dans la conception de l'Olympic Park lui-même, très différent de tout parc antérieur de ce type, nous ne créons pas un village olympique de plus qui ne serait qu'une série de jolis immeubles blancs et modernes sur un terrain plat. Nous créons quelque chose d'issu des conditions spécifiques et de la forme de la Lea Valley, et qui sera donc absolument unique. Les installations bénéficieront ensuite à la population locale. » La rénovation de la basse vallée de la Lea est d'une importance capitale pour la candidature britannique, et il est prévu que le village soit transformé en logements reliés par une nouvelle ligne de train au centre de Londres en sept minutes seulement. Le nouveau parc olympique de 225 hectares regroupera le stade olympique, le centre pour les jeux aquatiques, un vélodrome, trois salles de sport, un centre de hockey et des installations pour les médias, chaque équipement étant à sept minutes maximum l'un de l'autre. Le parc contiendra également le village olympique qui logera 17 800 sportifs et officiels directement en vue du stade olympique. Ce projet a nécessité quinze mois de travail et la collaboration de centaines de consultants, architectes, designers, experts en stades et sportifs.

Alejandro Zaero Polo of FOA has stated, "In the design of the Olympic Park ... We are creating something that will grow out of the specific conditions and form of the Lea Valley, making it totally unique. This will be part of the lasting legacy for the local community."

Alejandro Zaero Polo von FOA erklärte: „Mit dem Entwurf des Olympischen Parks ... schaffen wir etwas, das aus den spezifischen Bedingungen entstehen und das Lea Valley formen wird. Diese ganz einzigartige Situation wird Teil des bleibenden Erbes für die hiesige Kommune sein."

Alejandro Zaero Polo de FOA précise : « Avec ce projet de parc olympique ... nous créons quelque chose qui va se développer à partir des conditions et de la forme spécifiques de la Lea Valley pour devenir quelque chose d'unique ... qui fera partie du patrimoine des habitants de la région. »

#10

NORMAN FOSTER

FOSTER AND PARTNERS
Riverside Three
22 Hester Road
London SW11 4AN

Tel: +44 20 77 38 04 55
Fax: +44 20 77 38 11 07
e-mail:
enquiries@fosterandpartners.com
Web: www.fosterandpartners.com

Born in Manchester in 1935, **NORMAN FOSTER** studied Architecture and City Planning at Manchester University (1961). He was awarded a Henry Fellowship to Yale University, where he received his Masters of Architecture degree, and met Richard Rogers, with whom he created Team 4. He received the Royal Gold Medal for Architecture (1983), and was knighted in 1990. The American Institute of Architects granted him their Gold Medal for Architecture in 1994. Lord Norman Foster has notably built: the IBM Pilot Head Office, Cosham (1970–71); the Sainsbury Centre for Visual Arts and Crescent Wing, University of East Anglia, Norwich (1976–77; 1989–91); the Hong Kong and Shanghai Banking Corporation Headquarters, Hong Kong (1981–86); London's Third Airport, Stansted (1987–91); the University of Cambridge Faculty of Law, Cambridge (1993–95); and the Commerzbank Headquarters, Frankfurt (1994–97). Recent projects include: the Airport at Chek Lap Kok, Hong Kong (1995–98); the new German Parliament, Reichstag, Berlin (1995–99); and the British Museum Redevelopment, London (1997–2000). More recently the office completed the Greater London Authority (1998–2002); the Millennium Bridge, London (1996–2002) and the much larger Millau Viaduct in France (1993–2005); and 126 Philip Street, Sydney (1997–2005). Wembley Stadium, London (1996–2006), and Florence Station (2003-08) are underway.

30 ST MARY AXE
SWISS RE
HEADQUARTERS
LONDON
1997-2004

OFFICE AREA: 47 400 m²
Typical Floor area: 1400 m²
CLIENT: Swiss Re
COST: not disclosed

In many ways a new symbol of London, the new Swiss Re Headquarters is described by Foster as the "first environmental skyscraper." Natural ventilation is drawn up through the building's light wells. The same light-wells together with the shape of the building maximize natural light inside. Altogether, Foster's environmental emphasis means that the structure consumes "50 percent less energy than a traditional prestige office building." Its unusual curved exterior, designed with the aid of parametric modeling, has "an affinity with forms that recur in nature" according to the architects. The cladding, consisting of 5500 flat triangular and diamond-shaped glass panels for a total area of 24 000 m², gives an appearance that resembles a pinecone, for example. Actually built between 2001 and 2003, the structure has an office area of 46 000 m² on floors 2 to 34 and 1400 m² of retail space. With a total height of 180 meters, the tower has a top-floor restaurant, which at 165 meters above the ground is now London's highest. An upper level bar offers a 360° view of London. Norman Foster has long been interested in tall buildings and the completion of the Swiss Re Headquarters long after the events of September 11, 2001, in New York confirms the continuing vitality of this type of construction, particularly in dense urban areas.

Die in vielerlei Hinsicht als neues Symbol für London geltende neue Zentrale der Schweizer Rückversicherung wird von Foster als „erstes umweltgerechtes Hochhaus" bezeichnet. Die natürliche Be- und Entlüftung geschieht über die Lichtschächte des Gebäudes. Diese sorgen außerdem im Verbund mit der Gebäudeform für maximales Tageslicht im Inneren. Insgesamt bedeutet Fosters umweltgerechter Entwurf, dass der Bau „50 % weniger Energie verbraucht als ein herkömmliches, auf Prestige bedachtes Bürogebäude". Der ungewöhnliche, gerundete Außenbau, der mithilfe parametrischer Formgebung entstand, weist den Architekten zufolge „Ähnlichkeit mit in der Natur vorkommenden Formen" auf.

Durch die Verkleidung aus 5500 flachen dreieckigen und rautenförmigen Glasplatten auf 24 000 m² erinnert der Bau an einen Kiefernzapfen. Das Hochhaus verfügt auf den Stockwerken 2 bis 34 über 46 000 m² Büro- und zusätzlich über 1400 m² Ladenfläche. In einem der oberen Geschosse des insgesamt 180 m hohen Gebäudes befindet sich ein Restaurant, das mit 165 m über dem Boden zurzeit Londons höchstes Speiselokal ist. Eine Bar auf der oberen Ebene bietet einen 360-Grad-Rundblick auf London. Norman Foster ist seit langem an Hochhäusern interessiert, und die Fertigstellung der Zentrale der Swiss Re, lange nach den Ereignissen vom 11. September 2001 in New York, bekräftigt die anhaltende Vitalität dieses Bautyps, insbesondere in dicht bebauten Innenstädten.

Nouveau symbole de Londres à de nombreux égards, le siège de Swiss Re est décrit par Foster comme le « premier gratte-ciel environnemental ». Sa ventilation naturelle profite des puits de lumière qui, avec la forme particulière de l'immeuble, optimisent la pénétration de l'éclairage solaire. L'accent mis sur l'environnemental aboutit à ce que la tour « consomme 50 % moins d'énergie qu'un immeuble de bureaux de prestige traditionnel ». Sa curieuse forme incurvée a été conçue à l'aide de modèles paramétriques et présente « une affinité avec des formes trouvées dans la nature », selon l'architecte. L'habillage consiste en 5500 panneaux de verres triangulaires plats qui recouvrent 24 000 m² et donnent un aspect d'une pomme de pin. Édifiée entre 2001 et 2003, cette tour de 180 m de haut compte 46 000 m² de bureaux entre les niveaux 2 et 34 et 1400 m² réservés aux commerces. Un restaurant, le plus haut de Londres, se trouve à 165 m d'altitude et son bar offre une vue à 360° sur la capitale. Norman Foster s'intéresse depuis longtemps aux immeubles de grande hauteur et l'achèvement de la tour Swiss Re, longtemps après les événements du 11 septembre 2001, confirme la vitalité de ce type de construction, en particulier dans les zones urbaines denses.

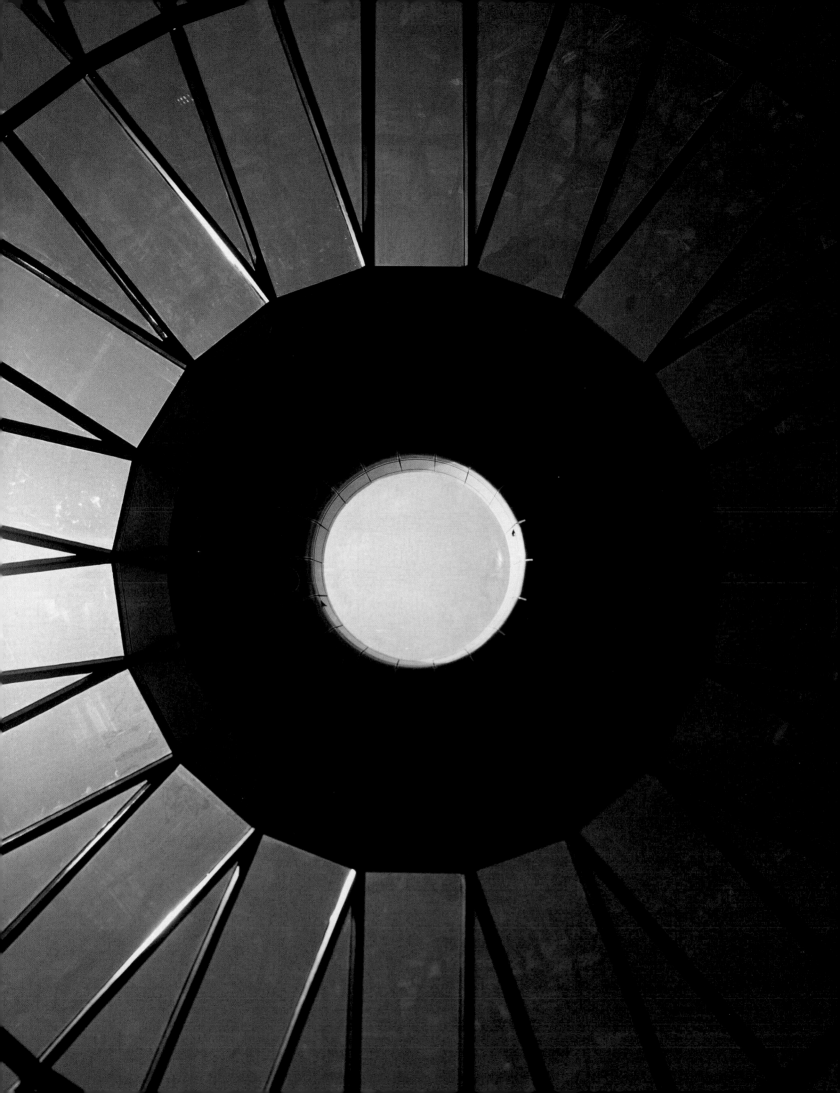

Foster's building has been compared to a number of objects, most frequently a gherkin, but in the view to the left, its striated bullet-like appearance dominates. Interior space, from the entrance to the upper level restaurant and bar, emphasizes the building's design continuity.

Man hat Fosters Gebäude mit einer Reihe von Objekten verglichen, am häufigsten mit einer Gurke, aber in der Ansicht links ist der Eindruck einer Patronenhülse beherrschend. Der Innenraum vom Eingang bis zu Restaurant und Bar auf der oberen Ebene unterstreicht sichtbar die Kontinuität des Entwurfs.

L'immeuble de Foster a été comparé à un certain nombre de choses – le plus souvent un cornichon – mais sur l'image de gauche, son aspect de balle de fusil striée prédomine. Le volume intérieur, de l'entrée jusqu'au restaurant et au bar du sommet, met en valeur la continuité du projet.

THE SAGE GATESHEAD 1997-2004

FLOOR AREA: 17 500 m²
CLIENT: Gateshead Council
COST: £70 million

This £70 million performing arts center sits on the River Tyne, next to the Tyne Bridge, looking toward Newcastle. Its most distinctive feature is a shell-like stainless-steel exterior. Three auditoriums, a music education center, entertainment rooms, a public concourse, and offices are all located under this roof. Supported by four 80-meter structural steel arches, the roof weighs 720 tons and is covered with 3000 linen-finish stainless-steel panels and 280 glass panels. As was the case in London for the Swiss Re tower, parametric modeling was used for the design of the roof and the manufacturing of the roof panels. Engineering was the responsibility of Buro Happold. Working with Arup Acoustics, the architects designed the performance halls, respectively seating 1700 and 400 persons, to the most exacting acoustical standards. Only the auditoriums are air conditioned, using the lowest possible airflow. The north-south orientation of the complex reduces solar gain, once again confirming Foster's ongoing interest in environmental issues. The structure has a gross floor area of 17 500 m² for a footprint of 8584 m². After an initial surge of one million visitors in 2005, The Sage Gateshead is expected to receive 600 000 visitors per year in the future.

Das für 70 Millionen Pfund erbaute Zentrum für darstellende Kunst liegt am River Tyne, in der Nähe der Tyne Bridge, und schaut in Richtung Newcastle. Sein prägnantestes Merkmal ist seine schalenförmige Außenhaut aus Edelstahl. Unter diesem Dach finden drei Auditorien, ein Zentrum für Musikerziehung, Veranstaltungsräume, eine öffentliche Promenade sowie Büroräume Platz. Das von vier 80 m hohen konstruktiven Stahlbögen gestützte Dach wiegt 720 t und ist von 3000 strukturierten Edelstahl- und 280 Glasplatten bedeckt. Ebenso wie beim Hochhaus der Swiss Re in London wurde auch hier für den Dachentwurf und die Fertigung der Dachplatten die parametrische Formgebung genutzt. Für die Bautechnik zeichnet Buro Happold verantwortlich. In Zusammenarbeit mit Arup Acoustics plante der Architekt die beiden Theatersäle mit 1700 bzw. 400 Sitzplätzen unter Beachtung der anspruchsvollsten akustischen Normen. Einzig die Auditorien sind klimatisiert, wenngleich mit dem geringstmöglichen Luftstrom. Die Nord-Süd-Ausrichtung des Komplexes verringert die Sonneneinstrahlung, eine weitere Bestätigung von Fosters anhaltendem Interesse an Fragen der Umweltverträglichkeit. Der Komplex verfügt bei einer Grundfläche von 8584 m² über eine Bruttogeschossfläche von 17 500 m². Nach dem Ansturm von einer Million Besuchern im Jahr 2005 erwartet man in „The Sage Gateshead" künftig 600 000 Besucher im Jahr.

Ce centre pour les arts qui a coûté 70 millions de livres se dresse au bord de la Tyne, près du Tyne Bridge, et regarde vers Newcastle. Sa caractéristique la plus notable est sa forme de coquillage. Trois auditoriums, un centre de formation à la musique, des espaces de réception, un vaste hall public et des bureaux sont regroupés sous son immense toiture. Soutenu par quatre arches en acier structurel de 80 m de long, ce toit de 720 tonnes est recouvert de 3000 panneaux d'acier de finition texturée et 280 panneaux de verre. Comme pour la tour Swiss Re à Londres, la modélisation paramétrique a servi à la conception de cette couverture et à la fabrication des panneaux. L'ingénierie était sous la responsabilité de Buro Happold. Les salles de spectacle, conçues en collaboration avec Arup Acoustics, comptent respectivement 1700 et 400 places bénéficiant d'un confort acoustique extraordinaire. Seules ces salles sont équipées d'une climatisation, qui minimise les flux d'air. L'orientation nord-sud du complexe a permis de diminuer le gain solaire, ce qui confirme une fois de plus l'intérêt de Foster pour les enjeux environnementaux. La construction offre 17 500 m² de surface brute et une emprise au sol de 8584 m². Après avoir reçu un million de visiteurs pour sa première année, en 2005, le Sage Gateshead en attend plus de 600 000 par an dans le futur.

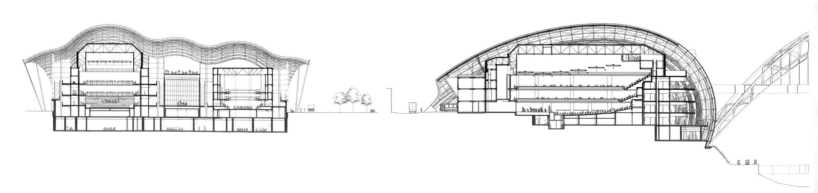

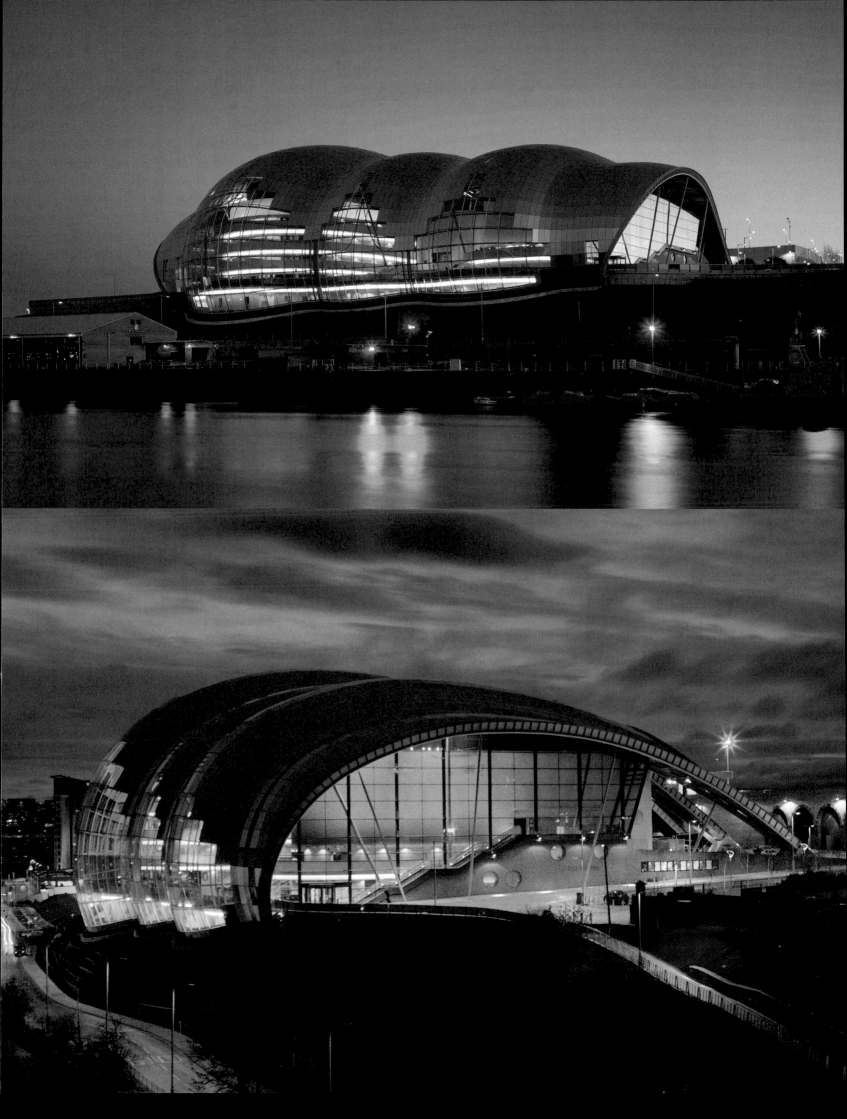

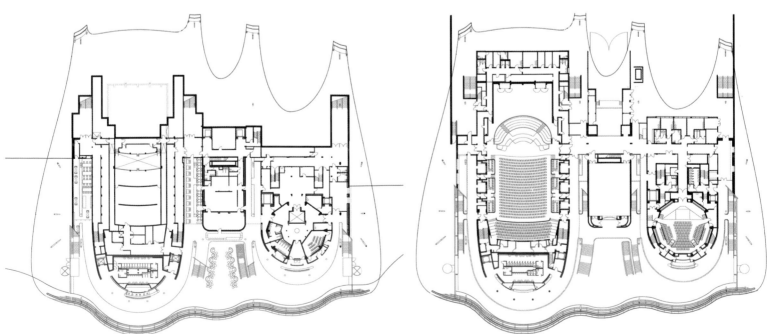

The wrapping form of the exterior shell allows for the creation of a spectacular interior space, while the plans to the left show how a fully functional layout is obtained despite the powerfully curved external envelope.

Die Schalenform der äußeren Hülle führt zu einem bemerkenswerten Innenraum. Der Grundriss links zeigt dagegen, wie trotz der spektakulär gebogenen Außenhaut ein gänzlich funktionales Layout erreicht wurde.

La forme enveloppante de la coque extérieure a permis de créer un volume intérieur spectaculaire. Les plans à gauche montrent comment un schéma pleinement fonctionnel a pu être obtenu malgré la forte présence de cette enveloppe incurvée.

The smaller hall, shown left and right, has an intimate feeling emphasized by coloring and lighting as well as the design itself, while the larger hall (above) has a considerably more substantial volume and an appearance of well-designed modern comfort.

Die links und auf der rechten Seite abgebildete kleinere Halle besitzt eine intime Atmosphäre, die durch Farbgebung, Beleuchtung und den Entwurf selbst unterstrichen wird. Die oben zu sehende größere Halle verfügt dagegen über ein beträchtlich größeres Volumen und bietet ein gut gestaltetes, modernes Ambiente.

La plus petite salle, à gauche et à droite, suscite un sentiment d'intimité mis en valeur par les couleurs et l'éclairage ainsi que par la conception elle-même. La grande salle (ci-dessus) dispose d'un volume beaucoup plus substantiel et offre un confort moderne agréablement pensé.

11

NICHOLAS GRIMSHAW

GRIMSHAW
1 Conway Street
Fitzroy Square
London W1T 6LR

Tel: +44 20 72 91 41 41
Fax: +44 20 72 91 41 94
e-mail: communications@
grimshaw-architects.com
Web: www.grimshaw-architects.com

A 1965 graduate of the Architectural Association (AA) in London, **NICHOLAS GRIMSHAW** was born in 1939 in London. He created the firm Nicholas Grimshaw and Partners Ltd. in 1980. His numerous factory structures include those built for Herman Miller in Bath (1976), BMW at Bracknell (1980), the furniture maker Vitra at Weil-am-Rhein, Germany (1981), and for *The Financial Times* in London in 1988. He also built houses associated with the Sainsbury Supermarket Development in Camden Town (1989), and the British Pavilion at the 1992 Universal Exhibition in Seville. One of his most visible works is the International Terminal of Waterloo Station, London (1988–93). Grimshaw currently employs a staff of 100 with offices in London, New York, and Melbourne. In 2001, it became the first major architectural firm to meet the Environmental Management System Standard BS EN ISO 14 001 and has since developed its own audit system, EVA or Environmentally Viable Architecture. Buildings completed in 2003 and 2004 include the Rolls Royce Manufacturing Plant and Head Office, Goodwest, West Sussex; University College London, Institute of Cancer Studies; Dubai Tower, Dubai; Fundación Caixa Galicia Arts and Cultural Centre, A Coruña, Spain; Sankei Nishiumeda Building, Osaka; University College London, New Engineering Building; and Zurich Airport, Switzerland.

BATH SPA
BATH
1997-2005

FLOOR AREA: 3650 m²
CLIENT: Bath & North East Somerset Council
Thermae Development Company
COST: not disclosed

The Bath Spa, one of four Millennium projects to have been designed by Grimshaw, was intended to revitalize the Spa quarter of the city, which fell into disuse twenty years ago. The firm was selected after an international design competition in 1997 that included 130 entries. Developed by the Bath & North East Somerset Council and Thermae Development Company, the project involves one new four-story building and the restoration of five other structures. The new structure includes a freestanding stone cube that holds pools, gymnasiums, and massage rooms. The architects point out that "dimensions of this cube relate directly to the plan of the neighboring Hot Bath building designed by John Wood in 1775." Bath Spa is the only functioning natural spa with hot-spring water in the UK. A restaurant, retail, and staff facilities in 7/7a Bath Street can be reached from an intermediate-level terraced area in the new building. Having been granted Planning & Listed Building Consent in 1999, the project started on site in September 2000, and was topped out in March 2002. The rather long delay between the competition and completion of the facility is undoubtedly due to the sensitive nature of the historic buildings involved. The fact that the complex was completed bears testimony to the capacity of Grimshaw to deal with the juxtaposition of modern and listed buildings.

Das „Bath Spa", eines von vier Millenniumsprojekten, für die Grimshaw verantwortlich zeichnet, sollte das seit 20 Jahren ungenutzte Kurviertel der Stadt mit neuem Leben erfüllen. Aus einem 1997 veranstalteten internationalen Wettbewerb, zu dem 130 Beiträge eingereicht worden waren, ging das Büro Grimshaw als Sieger hervor. Das vom Bath & North East Somerset Council und der Thermae Development Company geplante Projekt umfasst ein neues, viergeschossiges Gebäude sowie die Restaurierung von fünf weiteren Bauten. Zu dem Neubau gehört ein freistehender Steinkubus, in dem Schwimmbecken sowie Sport- und Massageräume untergebracht sind. Der Architekt wies darauf hin, dass „die Dimensionen dieses Kubus direkt Bezug nehmen auf den Grundriss des benachbarten, 1775 von John Wood erbauten Heißwasserbads". Beim Bath Spa handelt es sich um das einzige in Betrieb befindliche Bad mit natürlichem, heißem Quellwasser in Großbri-

tannien. Ein Restaurant, Ladengeschäfte sowie Einrichtungen für das Personal in der 7/7 a Bath Street erreicht man über ein terrassenförmig angelegtes Areal auf einer Zwischenebene im Neubau. Die Baugenehmigung und die Zustimmung der Denkmalbehörde für das Projekt erfolgten 1999, die Bauarbeiten begannen im September 2000, und das Richtfest wurde im März 2002 gefeiert. Der recht lange Zeitraum zwischen Wettbewerb und Fertigstellung der Anlage hängt zweifellos mit der Notwendigkeit eines sensiblen Umgangs mit den betroffenen historischen Bauten zusammen. Der Umstand, dass der Komplex inzwischen vollendet wurde, beweist überzeugend die Fähigkeit Grimshaws, mit dem Nebeneinander von moderner und denkmalgeschützter Bebauung umzugehen.

Le Bath Spa, nouvel établissement thermal figurant parmi les quatre projets financés dans le cadre des célébrations du Millenium, a été conçu par Grimshaw. L'objectif était de revitaliser les thermes locaux, abandonnés depuis vingt ans. L'agence a été sélectionnée à l'issue d'un concours international organisé en 1997, qui a attiré 130 participants. Financé par le Bath & North East Somerset Council et la Thermae Development Company, cette réalisation comprend un bâtiment neuf de quatre niveaux et la restauration de cinq autres constructions. Le nouveau Spa se compose d'un cube de pierre indépendant qui regroupe des piscines, des gymnases et des salles de massage. L'architecte fait remarquer que « les dimensions de ce cube évoquent directement le plan du bâtiment du Hot Bath dont les plans ont été dessinés par John Wood en 1775 ». Bath Spa est le seul établissement de bains fonctionnant à l'eau chaude naturelle au Royaume-Uni. Le restaurant, la boutique et les installations pour le personnel situés 7/7a Bath Street sont reliés au bâtiment neuf au niveau d'une terrasse intermédiaire de celui-ci. Après avoir obtenu son permis de construire dans une zone classée très protégée, le chantier a débuté en septembre 2000 et a été achevé en mars 2002. L'assez long délai entre le concours et l'ouverture est dû à la nature sensible des bâtiments historiques concernés. Le complexe achevé témoigne néanmoins de la capacité de Grimshaw à juxtaposer bâtiments modernes et historiques.

Inserting a clearly modern four-story cube into a traditional environment, the architect relies on simple lines and appropriate proportions. A section shows the relationship between the higher, new volume and a restored bath building to the left.

Beim Einfügen eines eindeutig modernen, vierstöckigen Kubus in ein traditionelles Umfeld setzt der Architekt auf schlichte Linienführung und passende Proportionen. Ein Schnitt zeigt die Beziehung zwischen dem höheren neuen Baukörper und dem restaurierten Badehaus auf der linken Seite.

En insérant un cube de quatre niveaux d'esprit résolument moderne dans un environnement traditionnel, l'architecte joue avec les lignes simples et les proportions appropriées. La coupe montre la relation entre le nouveau volume, plus élevé, et le bâtiment de bains ancien restauré, à gauche.

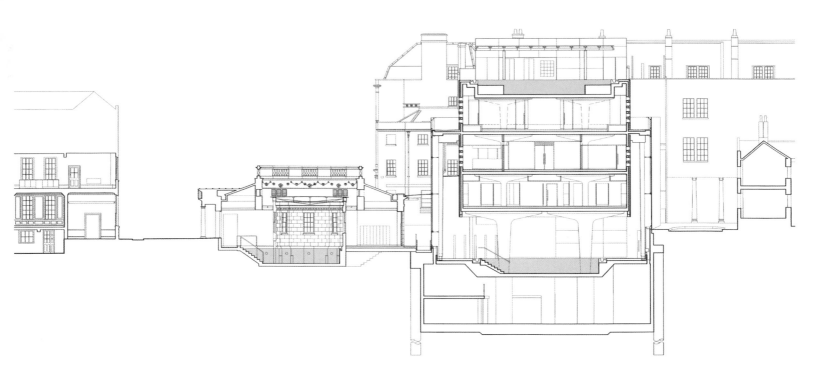

Curving, modern forms provide a contrast to the traditional architecture of the city and indeed to part of the restored structures themselves. Dealing with listed buildings, Grimshaw has resolved an extremely difficult equation without sacrificing his modern roots.

Gebogene, moderne Formen bilden einen Kontrast zur traditionellen Architektur der Stadt, ja selbst zu einem Teil der restaurierten Bebauung. Im Umgang mit denkmal-geschützten Bauten löste Grimshaw eine äußerst heikle Aufgabe, ohne seine eigene moderne Ausrichtung aufzugeben.

Les formes incurvées modernes contrastent avec l'architecture traditionnelle de la ville tout en s'intégrant aux constructions restaurées. Dans ce travail sur des immeubles classés, Grimshaw a résolu une équation extrêmement délicate sans sacrifier sa culture moderne.

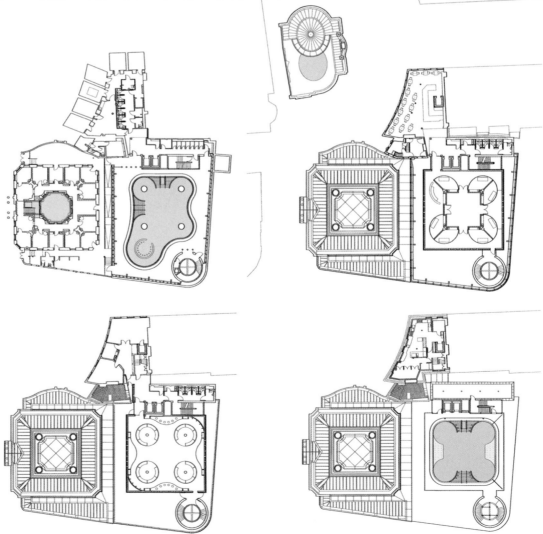

EDEN PROJECT
BODELVA, CORNWALL 1998-2005

FLOOR AREA: Biomes and Link Building: 23 000 m²;
Dry Tropics Biome, Education Center
and Visitor Gateway: 14 890 m²
Eden Foundation: 1800 m²
CLIENT: Eden Project Ltd.
COST: Biomes and Link Building: £57 million; Dry
Tropics Biome, Education Center
and Visitor Gateway: £9 million
Eden Foundation: £2,3 million

This very unusual project is intended as a "showcase for global bio-diversity and human dependence upon plants." The first phase, completed in 2001, was made up of 23 000 m² of "linked, climate-controlled transparent capsules (biomes) set in a design landscape." The budget for this project, which made use of the same consultants who worked on Grimshaw's very successful Waterloo International Terminal, was £57 million. Although its objectives might be considered as more far-reaching, this scheme does bring to mind the Yamanashi Museum of Fruit designed by Itsuko Hasegawa in Japan, which is also made up of a series of greenhouse structures. The domes in St Austell are to be based on lightweight structures with the highest possible volume vis-à-vis their surface. The cladding is made up of "optically clear air inflated foil (ETFE or Ethylene Tetra Fluoro Ethylene) pillows." The whole is intended to "give the impression of a biomorphic organism." As the architects say, "The final scheme represents the perfect fulfillment of Buckminster Fuller's vision—the maximum enclosed volume within the minimal surface area." The Visitors' Center, opened on May 15, 2000, is "primarily an educational facility, housing multimedia exhibits that introduce the aims and objectives of the project. It curves dramatically, complementing the contours of the quarry." Intended for 645 000 visitors a year, the Eden Project attracted 1.956 million in its first year of operation. The Eden Foundation Building, built to an entirely PVC-free specification, is a 1800 m² structure with a contract value of £2.5 million and was completed in 2002. The Dry Tropics Biome, Education Centre and Visitor Gateway, a £9 million, 14 890 m² series of additions to the original Buildings, was due for completion in 2005.

Dieses außergewöhnliche Projekt ist angelegt als „Schaukasten der weltweiten biologischen Vielfalt und der menschlichen Abhängigkeit von Pflanzen". Der 2001 fertig gestellte erste Abschnitt besteht aus 23 000 m² „miteinander verbundener, klimatisierter, transparenter Kuppeln, so genannte Biomes, die in eine gestaltete Landschaft eingefügt sind". Das Budget für dieses Projekt, zu dem die gleichen Berater herangezogen wurden wie zu Grimshaws äußerst gelungenem International Terminal am Bahnhof Waterloo, betrug 57 Millionen Pfund. Obgleich die Zielsetzung hier sehr viel umfassender ist, erinnert die Anlage doch an das von Itsuko Hasegawa entworfene Yamanashi Museum of Fruit, das ebenfalls aus einer Abfolge von Gewächshausbauten besteht. Die Kuppeln in St. Austell basieren auf Leichtbaukonstruktionen mit dem im Verhältnis zu ihrer Oberfläche größtmöglichen Rauminhalt. Die Verkleidung besteht aus „durchsichtigen, luftgefüllten Folienkissen (ETFE oder Ethylentetrafluorethylen)". Das Ganze soll „den Eindruck eines biomorphen Organismus" hervorrufen. Der Architekt erläutert: „Der endgül-

tige Entwurf stellt die perfekte Erfüllung von Buckminster Fullers Vision dar – maximaler Rauminhalt bei minimaler Oberfläche." Bei dem am 15. Mai 2000 eröffneten Besucherzentrum „handelt es sich in erster Linie um eine Lehreinrichtung mit multimedialen Exponaten, die in die Ziele des Projekts einführen. Seine spektakulär geschwungene und gerundete Architektur passt sich den Umrisslinien der ehemaligen Kaolingrube an." Das für 645 000 Besucher pro Jahr ausgelegte Eden-Projekt zog im ersten Jahr nach seiner Eröffnung 1,9 Millionen Menschen an. Das 2002 fertig gewordene Gebäude der Eden Foundation mit Baukosten von 2,5 Millionen Pfund kommt gänzlich ohne die Verwendung von PVC aus und umfasst 1800 m². Die Fertigstellung des „Bioms der trockenen Tropen" sowie des Lernzentrums und Besuchereingangs ist für 2005 vorgesehen. Die Kosten für diese Ergänzungsbauten mit einer Fläche von insgesamt 14 890 m² sind mit 9 Millionen Pfund veranschlagt.

Ce très curieux projet se veut « une vitrine de la biodiversité globale et de la dépendance de l'homme par rapport aux plantes ». Sa première phase, achevée en 2001, se compose de 23 000 m² de « capsules transparentes » (biomes) interconnectées, à microclimat contrôlé, implantées dans un paysage aménagé. Le budget de ce projet, qui a fait appel aux mêmes consultants que ceux qui avaient collaboré avec Grimshaw au Terminal international de Waterloo, s'est élevé à 57 millions de livres. Bien que ces objectifs puissent sembler très éloignés, cette entreprise rappelle le Musée du fruit de Yamanashi, conçu par Itsuko Hasegawa au Japon, également composé d'une série de serres. Les dômes de St Austell sont faites de structures légères offrant le plus grand volume possible par rapport à leur surface. L'habillage est en « oreillers en film optiquement transparent (en ETFE ou éthylène tétra fluoro ethylène) gonflé ». L'ensemble donne « l'impression d'un organisme biomorphique ». Pour l'architecte : « La réalisation finale représente l'accomplissement parfait de la vision de Buckminster Fuller, le plus grand volume clos possible sous la surface couvrante la plus réduite possible. » Le Centre d'accueil des visiteurs, ouvert le 15 mai 2000, est « essentiellement un centre éducatif abritant des présentations multimédias qui expliquent les buts et objectifs du projet. Sa courbure spectaculaire se fond dans les contours de la carrière. » Prévu pour 645 000 visiteurs annuels, le projet Eden en a attiré près de 2 millions la première année. Le bâtiment de la Eden Foundation, construit selon un programme entièrement sans PVC, est une construction de 1800 m² de 2,5 millions de livres, achevée en 2002. Le biome des tropiques secs, le centre éducatif et la porte des visiteurs, programme d'extension de 14 890 m² et de 9 millions de livres, devraient être achevés en 2005.

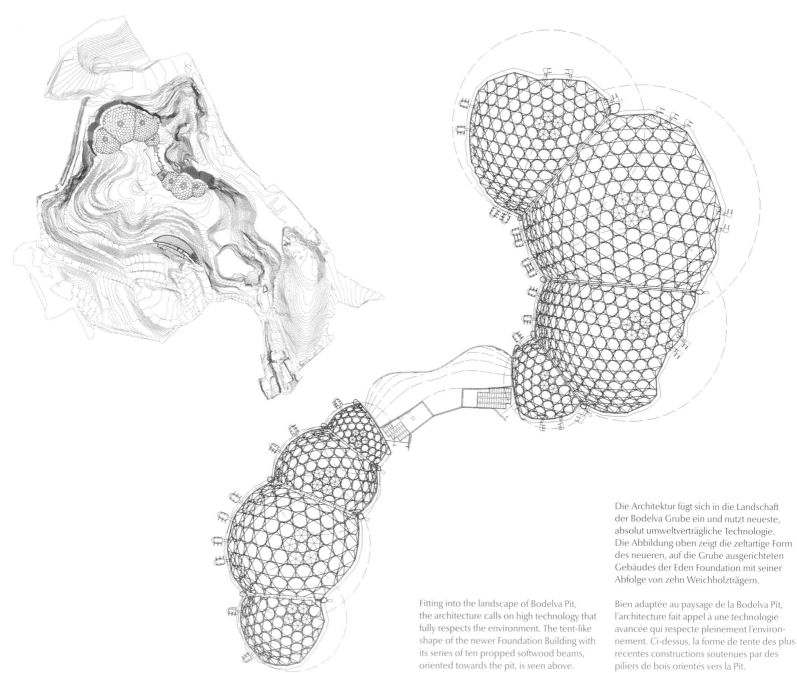

Die Architektur fügt sich in die Landschaft der Bodelva Grube ein und nutzt neueste, absolut umweltverträgliche Technologie. Die Abbildung oben zeigt die zeltartige Form des neueren, auf die Grube ausgerichteten Gebäudes der Eden Foundation mit seiner Abfolge von zehn Weichholzträgern.

Fitting into the landscape of Bodelva Pit, the architecture calls on high technology that fully respects the environment. The tent-like shape of the newer Foundation Building with its series of ten propped softwood beams, oriented towards the pit, is seen above.

Bien adaptée au paysage de la Bodelva Pit, l'architecture fait appel à une technologie avancée qui respecte pleinement l'environnement. Ci-dessus, la forme de tente des plus récentes constructions soutenues par des piliers de bois orientés vers la Pit.

The very large volume of the PVC-free domes is in fact the result of imagined spherical shapes as the drawing below shows. Derived from Buckminster Fuller's geodesic designs, the domes cover a maximum area with a minimum amount of structural material.

Wie die Zeichnung unten zeigt, ist das äußerst umfangreiche Volumen der PVC-freien Kuppeln tatsächlich von gedachten sphärischen Formen abgeleitet. Inspiriert von Buckminster Fullers geodätischen Entwürfen, überdecken die Kuppeln eine maximale Fläche mit dem geringstmöglichen Einsatz konstruktiven Materials.

Le très grand volume des coupoles en matériau sans PVC vient en fait de formes sphériques imaginées, comme le montre le dessin ci-dessous. Inspirées des dômes géodésiques de Buckminster Fuller, elles recouvrent une surface maximum pour une quantité minimale de matériaux.

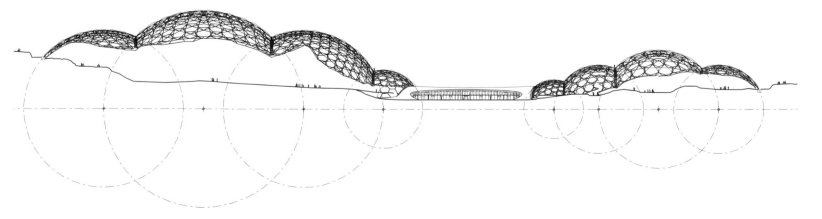

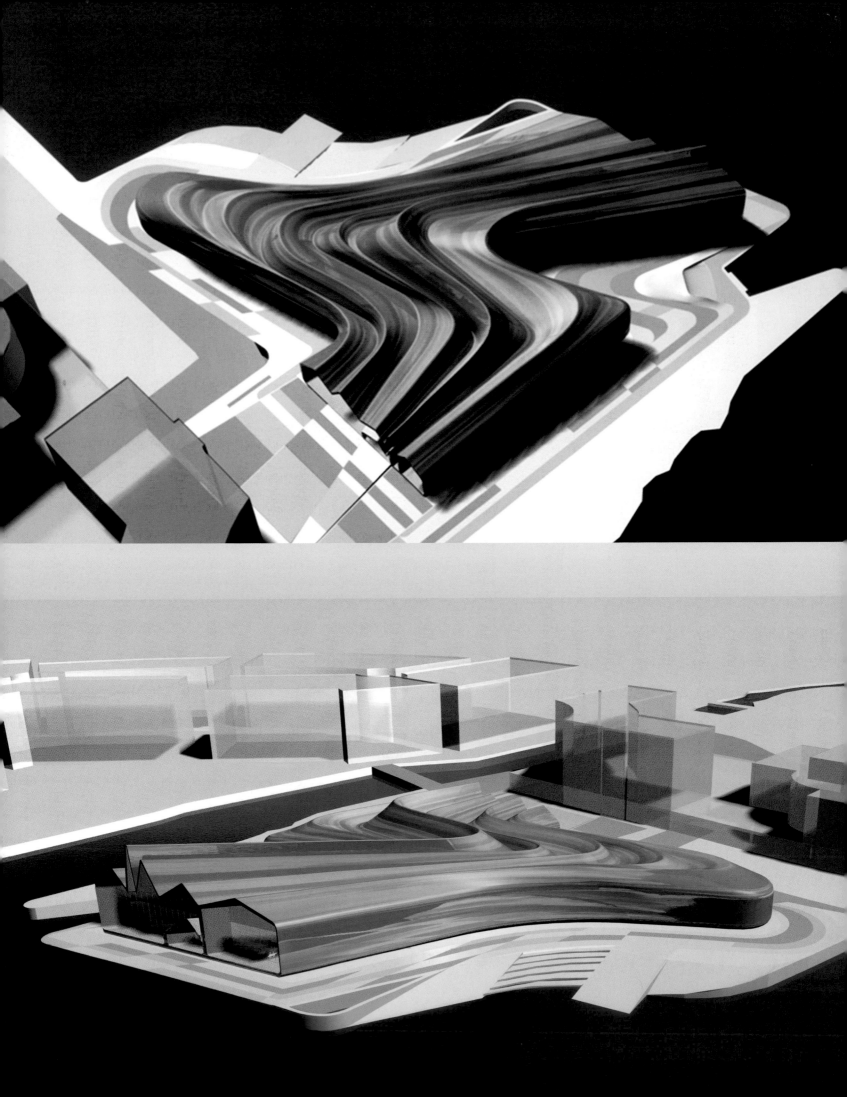

12

ZAHA HADID

ZAHA HADID ARCHITECTS
Studio 9
10 Bowling Green Lane
London EC1R OBQ

Tel: +44 20 72 53 51 47
Fax: +44 20 72 51 83 22
e-mail: mail@zaha-hadid.com
Web: www.zaha-hadid.com

ZAHA HADID studied architecture at the Architectural Association (AA) in London, beginning in 1972, and was awarded the Diploma Prize in 1977. She then became a partner of Rem Koolhaas in the Office for Metropolitan Architecture (OMA) and taught at the AA. She has also taught at Harvard, the University of Chicago, in Hamburg, and at Columbia University in New York. Well known for her paintings and drawings, she has had a substantial influence, despite having built relatively few buildings. She has completed the Vitra Fire Station, Weil-am-Rhein, Germany (1990–94), and exhibition designs such as that for "The Great Utopia," Solomon R. Guggenheim Museum, New York, 1992. Significant competition entries include her design for the Cardiff Bay Opera House (1994–96); the Habitable Bridge, London (1996); and the Luxembourg Philharmonic Hall, Luxembourg (1997). More recently, Zaha Hadid has entered a phase of active construction with such projects as the Bergisel Ski Jump, Innsbruck (2001–02); Lois & Richard Rosenthal Center for Contemporary Art, Cincinnati, Ohio (1999–2003); and the Central Building of the new BMW Assembly Plant in Leipzig (2005). She is working on the Price Tower Arts Center, Bartlesville, Oklahoma; Doha Tower, Doha, Qatar; and made a proposal for the 2012 Olympic Village, New York. In 2004, Zaha Hadid became the first woman to win the coveted Pritzker Prize.

GLASGOW MUSEUM OF TRANSPORT
GLASGOW 2004-08

FLOOR AREA: 10 000 m²
CLIENT: Glasgow City Council
COST: £50 million

To be built for the City Council at 22 Trongate in Glasgow, this 10 000 m² museum will have 7000 m² of exhibition space. The architects speak of a "wave" or a "pleated movement" in describing the building, which will have a café and corporate entertainment space at one end with a view on the River Clyde. As they describe it, "The building would be a tunnel-like shed, which is open at opposite ends to the city and the Clyde. In doing so it becomes porous to its context on either side. However, the connection from one to the other is where the building diverts to create a journey away from the external context into the world of the exhibits. Here the interior path becomes a mediator between the city and the river which can either be hermetic or porous depending on the exhibition layout. Thus the museum positions itself symbolically and functionally as open and fluid with its engagement of context and content." The office has also proposed a landscape scheme for the surrounding area, which would ring the building with stone slabs of varying size. An informal grass courtyard area would be located on the west side of the building, while a line of trees would reduce wind exposure on the existing ferry quay. Shallow ponds to the south and east would emphasize the continuity of the building with the Clyde. One of a number of projects by recognized architects in Glasgow, the Museum of Transport Riverside Project underlines the desire of the city to confirm and develop its position as the cultural capital of Scotland.

Dieses Museum mit 10 000 m² Fläche, davon 7000 m² Ausstellungsfläche, soll im Auftrag des City Council von Glasgow an der Trongate 22 in Glasgow entstehen. Wenn sie das Gebäude beschreiben, sprechen die Architekten von einer „Welle" oder von „gefalteter Bewegung". An einem Ende des Museums werden ein Café sowie Veranstaltungsräume für Firmen mit Blick auf den River Clyde untergebracht sein. Der Beschreibung nach wird es sich bei dem Museum um einen „tunnelartigen Schuppen handeln, der an den entgegengesetzten Enden zur Stadt und zum Fluss hin offen und so nach beiden Seiten zu seinem Umfeld hin durchlässig ist. Gleichwohl fügt der Bau bei der Verbindung von der einen zur anderen Seite einen Umweg ein, um den Besucher weg von der Umgebung in die Welt der Exponate zu führen. Hier wird der innere Weg zu einem Mittler zwischen Stadt

und Fluss, der, abhängig vom Grundriss der Ausstellung, entweder geschlossen oder durchlässig sein kann. Somit zeigt sich das Museum symbolisch und funktional als offen und flexibel in der Interaktion mit Kontext und Inhalt." Das Büro hat außerdem einen Plan für die Gestaltung der Umgebung entwickelt, der vorsieht, den Bau mit Steinplatten unterschiedlicher Größe zu umgeben. Auf der westlichen Seite des Museums ist ein begrünter Innenhof geplant, während eine Baumreihe am bestehenden Fähranleger den Wind abhalten soll. Flache Wasserbecken im Süden und Osten sollen den Bezug des Gebäudes zum Fluss unterstreichen. Als ein Beitrag in einer Reihe von Projekten namhafter Architekten in Glasgow unterstreicht das Museum of Transport den Wunsch der Stadt, ihre Stellung als kulturelle Hauptstadt Schottlands zu stärken und auszubauen.

Construit pour la ville de Glasgow sur un terrain situé 22 Trongate, ce musée de 10 000 m² offrira 7000 m² d'espaces d'exposition. L'architecte parle d'une « vague » ou d'un « mouvement de plis » pour décrire ce projet qui prévoit également un café et des espaces de réception donnant sur la River Clyde. « Le bâtiment sera un shed en forme de tunnel ouvert à ses deux extrémités opposées, vers la ville et la Clyde. Ce faisant, il devient poreux par rapport à son contexte, des deux côtés. Cependant, la connexion de l'un à l'autre est là où le projet se distingue pour créer une promenade loin du contexte externe, dans le monde même de l'exposition. Le cheminement intérieur se transforme en médiateur entre la ville et le fleuve, médiateur qui peut être soit hermétique soit poreux selon le plan de l'exposition. Ainsi le musée se positionne symboliquement et fonctionnellement comme ouvert et fluide dans sa mise en jeu du contexte et du contenu. » L'agence a également proposé un projet d'aménagement paysager pour le terrain qui entoure le musée à base de dalles de pierre de tailles diverses. Une cour informelle sera plantée de gazon à l'ouest, tandis qu'une rangée d'arbres abritera du vent du côté du quai des ferries. Au sud et à l'est, des bassins mettront en valeur la continuité du bâtiment avec la Clyde. Ce projet fait partie d'un programme confié par Glasgow à des architectes connus. Il souligne le désir de la ville de confirmer et de développer sa position de capitale culturelle de l'Écosse.

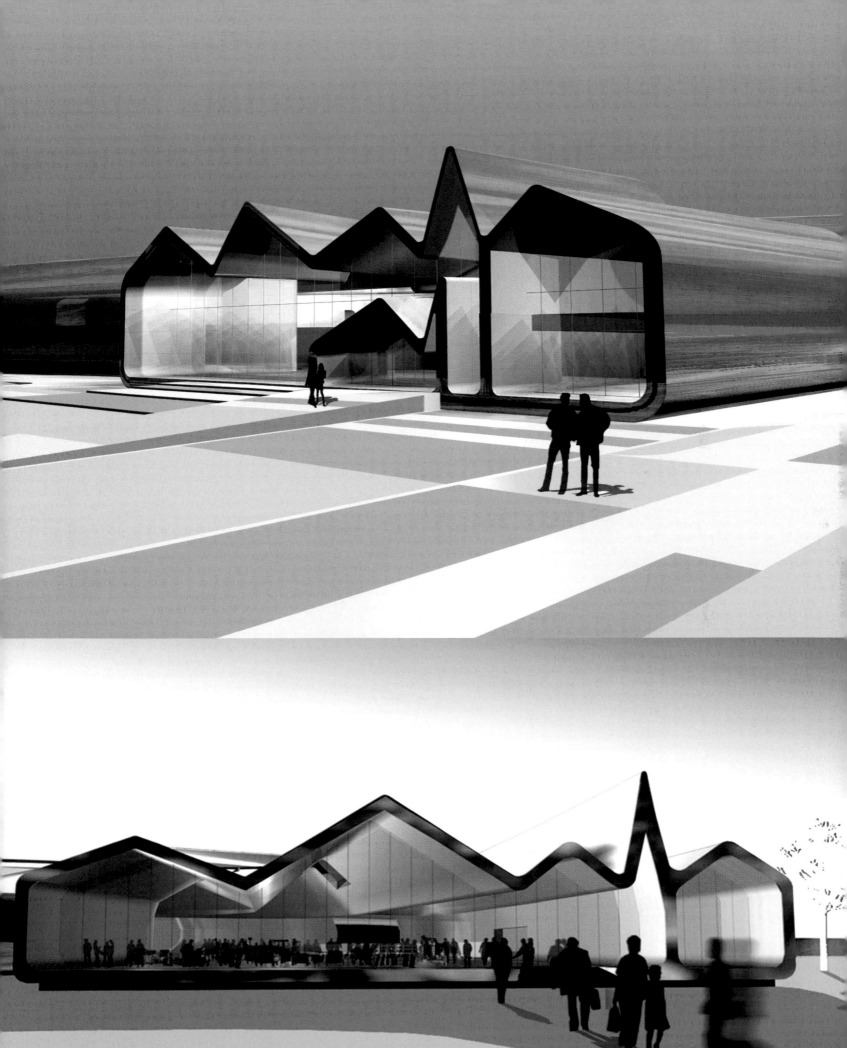

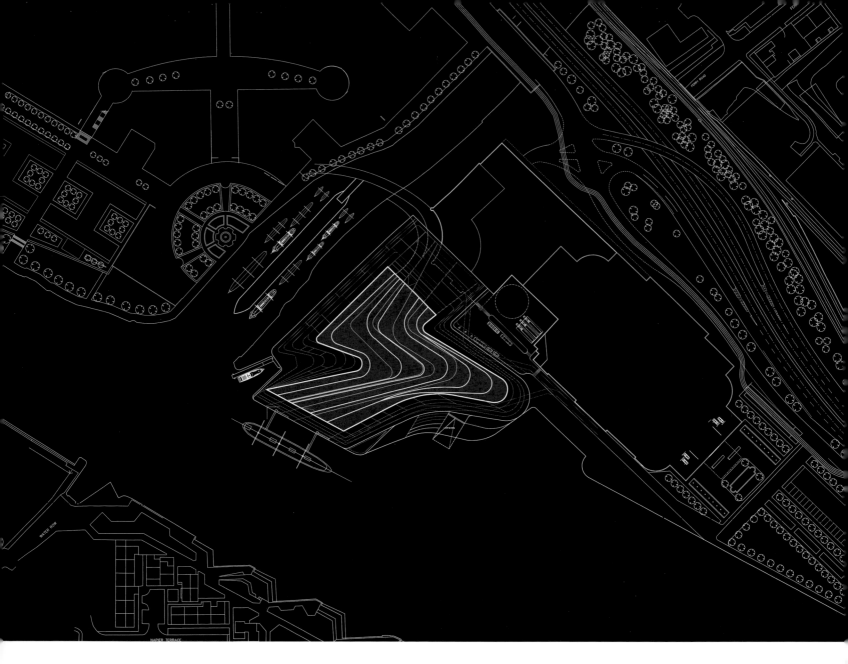

The wrapping, wave-like or topographically influenced shape of the building is seen in a site plan above and sections below that reveal the large column-free spaces created within the unusual exterior shell.

Die gewickelte, wellenartige oder topographisch bedingte Gebäudeform ist auf einem Geländeplan (oben) und Schnitten (unten) zu sehen. Man erkennnt die Räume, die in dieser ungewöhnlichen äußeren Hülle geschaffenen wurden.

Dans le plan ci-dessus et les coupes ci-dessous, l'enveloppement en vague ou influencé par la topographie du lieu et les vastes volumes dégagés de toute colonne créés par l'étonnante coque extérieure.

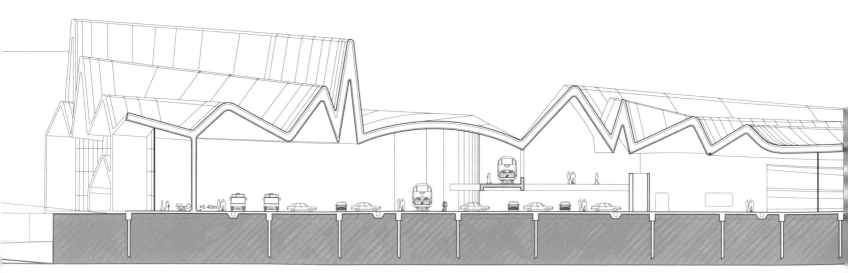

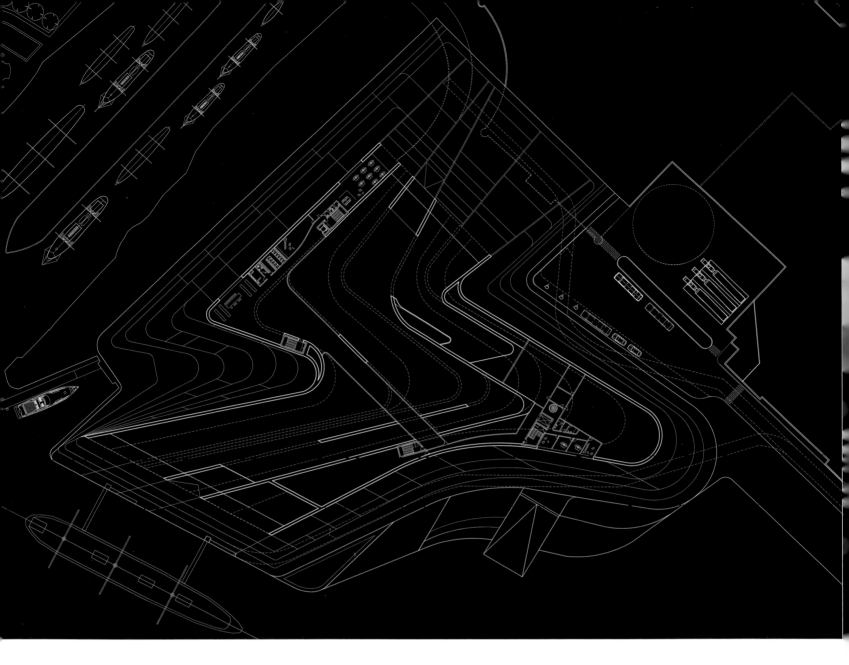

Plan and section again show a building that appears to flow into its site naturally, almost effortlessly creating the wide-span exhibition areas required in this instance.

Grundriss und Schnitt zeigen erneut ein Gebäude, das ganz natürlich auf seinen Platz zu gleiten scheint und dabei nahezu mühelos die in diesem Fall erforderlichen großräumigen Ausstellungsflächen schafft.

Un plan et une coupe montrent le projet semblant suspendu au-dessus de son site, générant presque sans effort les aires d'exposition à couverture de grande portée.

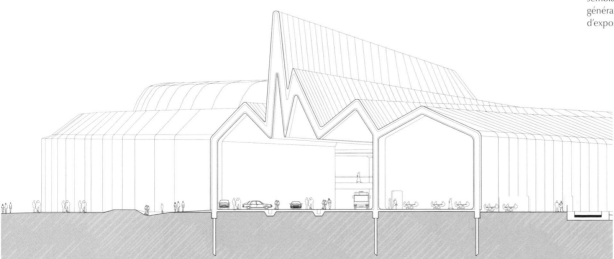

ARCHITECTURE FOUNDATION BUILDING

LONDON 2005-

FLOOR AREA: 640 m^2
CLIENT: Architecture Foundation
COST: not disclosed

This new 640 m^2 structure for the Architecture Foundation is to include 300 m^2 of exhibition space, a café, and offices. It is to be located at 60 Bastwick Street in London. As the architects describe the project, "A solid concrete ribbon is folded over itself to generate the structural lining of the building. This ribbon of continuous structure wraps itself around a full height atrium which is delineated by a transparent envelope of glass. The dichotomy between the powerful sculptural mass of the structure and the visual permeability of the envelope creates a bold and emblematic frame of natural light and shadow that serves as a portal for maintaining both visual and pedestrian connections through the building and its site." An atrium in the center is meant to be a flexible space allowing for installations or the exhibition of large-scale architectural models or other objects. Office space is located on the first floor. A bar opens out to the exhibition space and the exterior, emphasizing the overall theme of transparency and openness of the interior toward the exterior and vice-versa.

In diesem 640 m^2 umfassenden Neubau der Architecture Foundation sollen 300 m^2 Ausstellungsfläche, ein Café und Büros Platz finden. Er soll an der Bastwick Street 60 in London errichtet werden. Die Architekten beschreiben das Projekt folgendermaßen: „Ein kompaktes Betonband wird doppelt gefaltet, um die konstruktive Verkleidung des Gebäudes zu bilden. Dieses kontinuierliche Band bestimmt die Form des Gebäudes und windet sich um ein Atrium in voller Höhe, das durch eine transparente Glashülle umschrieben ist. Der Gegensatz zwischen der plastischen Gebäudemasse und der visuellen Durchlässigkeit der Hülle erzeugt einen kühnen, emblematischen Rahmen aus Tageslicht und Schatten, der als Portal für Passanten dient, die den Bau und sein Gelände mit Blicken oder zu Fuß durchstreifen." Das zentrale Atrium ist als flexibler Raum gedacht, sowohl für Installationen wie für die Präsentation großformatiger Architekturmodelle oder anderer Objekte. Die Büroräume sind im ersten Geschoss untergebracht. Eine Bar ist zum Ausstellungsraum und zum Außenraum hin geöffnet und unterstreicht damit das übergreifende Thema von Transparenz und Offenheit zwischen Gebäudeinnerem und Außenraum.

Ce nouvel immeuble de 640 m^2 projeté pour l'Architecture Foundation, 60 Bastwick Street à Londres, comprendra 300 m^2 d'espaces d'exposition, un café et des bureaux. L'architecte le décrit ainsi : « Un ruban de béton massif replié sur lui-même pour créer une doublure structurelle du bâtiment. Ruban continu, il entoure un atrium toute hauteur délimité par une enveloppe de verre transparente. La dichotomie entre la puissante masse sculpturale de la structure et la perméabilité visuelle de son enveloppe crée un cadre emblématique de lumière naturelle et d'ombre qui sert de portail d'accès aux connexions à la fois visuelles et de circulation à travers le bâtiment et son site. » L'atrium central est un espace flexible qui permet l'installation d'expositions de maquettes architecturales à grande échelle ou d'autres pièces. Les bureaux sont situés au premier niveau. Un bar s'ouvre à la fois sur l'espace d'exposition et vers l'extérieur, illustrant là aussi le thème d'ensemble de transparence et d'ouverture dedans-dehors, fonctionnant dans les deux sens.

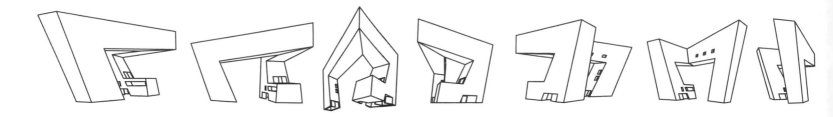

The main structural element of the building is a folded or bent concrete band, wrapped around the fully glazed atrium. The drawings above emphasize the sculptural quality of the design, the building appears under some angles to be in a delicate equilibrium.

Das statische Hauptelement des Gebäudes ist ein gefaltetes oder gebogenes Band aus Beton, das um ein vollverglastes Atrium verläuft. Die Zeichnungen (oben) verdeutlichen die skulpturale Qualität des Entwurfs; aus einigen Blickwinkeln scheint das Gebäude fast aus dem Gleichgewicht zu geraten.

Le principal élément structurel est un bandeau en béton, cintré, replié, qui enveloppe l'atrium entièrement vitré. Les dessins ci-dessus font ressortir la qualité sculpturale du projet qui, vu sous certains angles, semble frôler un équilibre délicat.

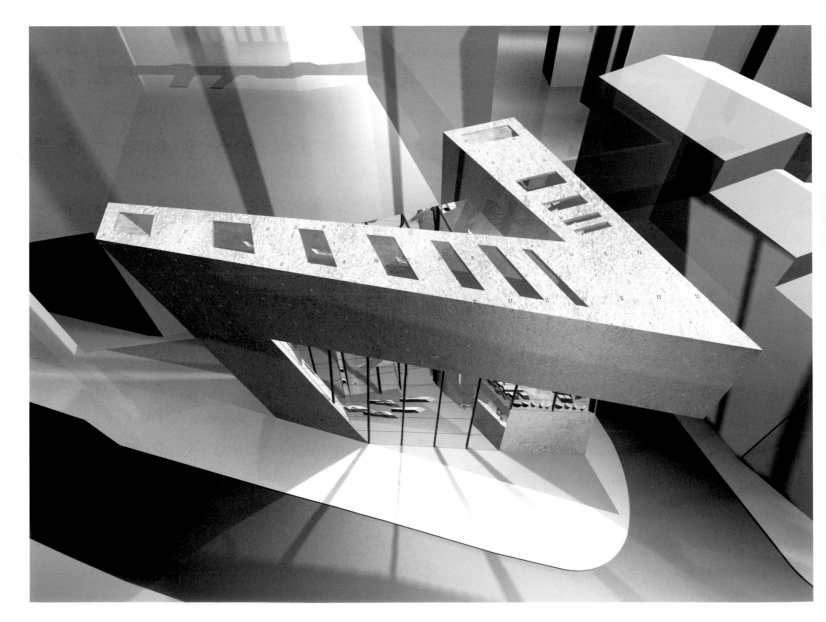

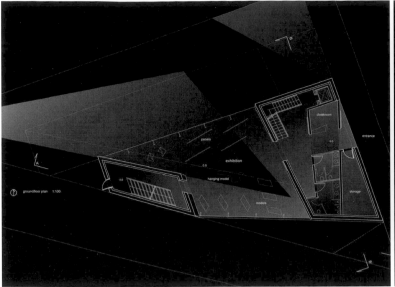

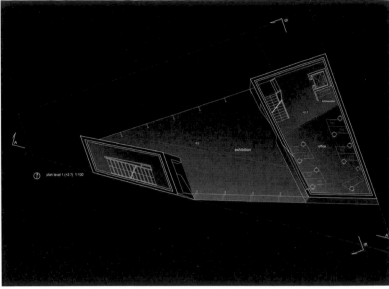

In section and plan, the audacious tilting form of the architecture resolves itself into a small but very flexible space, open in large part to the outside, fully visible from the exterior.

In Schnitt und Grundriss verwandelt sich die kühn gekippte Gebäudeform in einen kleinen, sehr flexiblen Raum, der größtenteils zum Außenraum offen ist und von außen vollständig eingesehen werden kann.

En coupe et en plan, l'audacieuse forme inclinée de l'architecture se résume en un volume petit mais très flexible, ouvert en grande partie sur l'extérieur d'où il est pleinement visible.

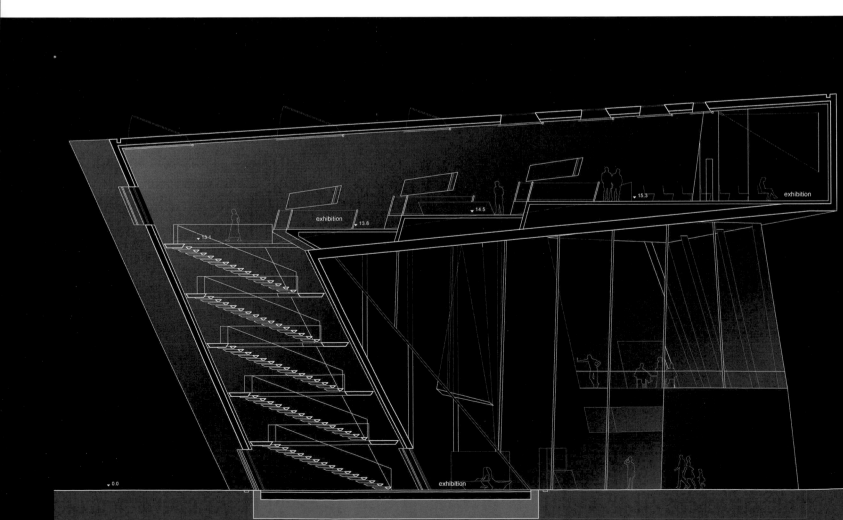

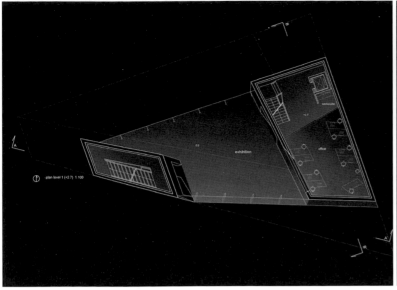

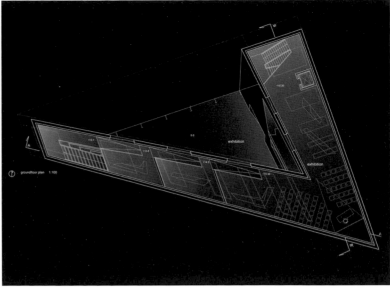

The cantilevered block contains an exhibition area, "where a succession of spaces of various scales allows for a variety of uses, such as multimedia exhibitions or talks and debates."

Der auskragende Gebäudeteil enthält einen Ausstellungsbereich, „in dem dank einer Folge von Räumen verschiedener Größe eine Vielzahl von Nutzungen wie Multimedia-Ausstellungen, Vorträge oder Diskussionsrunden möglich ist."

Les blocs en porte-à-faux contiennent un espace d'exposition « où une succession d'espaces d'échelles diverses permettent des utilisations variées comme des expositions multimédias, des conférences ou des débats ».

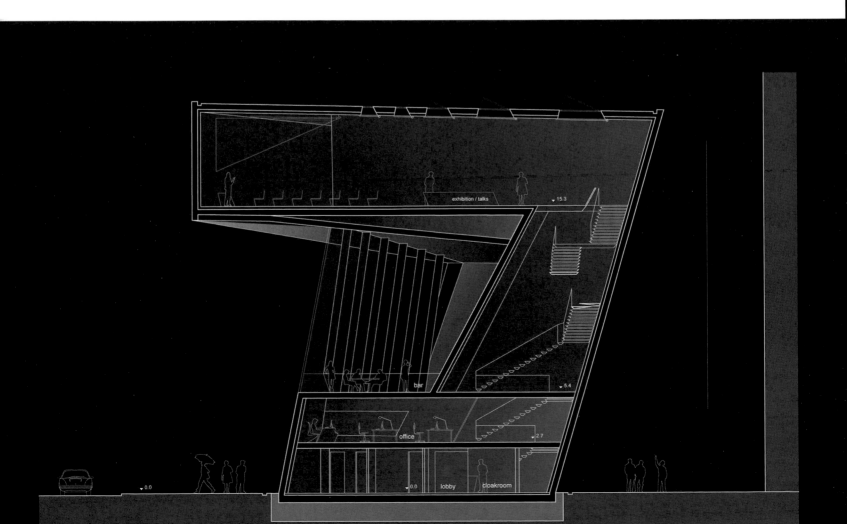

13

MICHAEL HOPKINS

HOPKINS ARCHITECTS
27 Broadley Terrace
London NW1 6LG

Tel: +44 20 77 24 17 51
Fax: +44 20 77 23 09 32
e-mail: mail@hopkins.co.uk
Web: www.hopkins.co.uk

MICHAEL HOPKINS was born in 1935, in Poole, Dorset, and studied architecture at the London Architecture Association (AA), graduating with a Diploma in 1964. He worked subsequently with Leonard Manasseh on the design of new halls of residence at Leicester University. In 1968 he worked with Norman and Wendy Foster on a plan to build an industrial estate at Goole in Yorkshire. Their partnership lasted eight years. In 1976, he founded his own firm. Some of his significant buildings include: Schlumberger Research Center, Cambridge (1979–81); The Mound Stand, St John's Wood, London (1985–87); Inland Revenue Headquarters, Nottingham (1993); Glyndebourne Opera House (1994); and the Parliamentary Office, Portcullis House, London (2001). He won RIBA's Royal Gold Medal in 1994 together with his wife, who is also an architect. The practice's more recent commissions include the master plan for a town center development in Chester; the master plan for Suffolk University; Norwich Cathedral Education and Visitors Centre; Greene King Brewery Distribution Depot; and the redevelopment of the Norwich library site. As the architects describe their practice, "Our goal at Hopkins Architects is to design innovative, cost effective and beautiful buildings that enable clients to make the most of their site, program and budget. We create logical and clear designs starting from our clients' needs, using the principles of 'truth to materials and expression of structure,' from which stems aesthetic quality, efficiency and popular appeal of our buildings. Since we started in 1976, we have pioneered a series of strategies including fabric roofs, lightweight structures, energy efficient design, weaving new structures into existing ones, and recycling brown land." Other recent work includes: Inn the Park, St James's Park, London (2004), and the GEK Group Headquarters, Athens (2003).

WELLCOME TRUST GIBBS BUILDING

LONDON 1999-2004 REFURBISHMENT 2006

FLOOR AREA: New headquarters: 28 000 m^2;
Refurbishment: 16 700 m^2
CLIENT: The Wellcome Trust
COST: £90 million

The Wellcome Trust is one of the largest charities in the world. Created on the basis of the will of Sir Henry Wellcome in 1936, the mission of the Trust is "to foster and promote research with the aim of improving human and animal health." The new headquarters of the Trust, designed by Hopkins Architects, is intended to bring the staff of 600 into a single site at 183–215 Euston Road in London. The new 28 000 m^2 building is situated next to the Trust's former Greek Revival premises designed by Septimus Warwick in the 1930s, which are to be refurbished. The library, exhibition space, lecture and conference facilities will be situated in this space, being redesigned by Hopkins to bring daylight deeper into the 16 700 m^2 building. "The work," say the architects, "will re-establish the legibility of the existing building and create a clear hierarchy of public and private spaces." In the new building, which is almost entirely clad in glass, two blocks, respectively facing Euston Road and Gower Place to the south, are joined together by a curving roof and an atrium. A series of formal meeting rooms, an internal street, staff café, information center, and more informal meeting areas constitute the ground floor. Both new blocks have offices in their upper levels with a restaurant on top of the southern volume. Despite careful attention to details, the cost of this project, at about £3000 per square meter, is considered exemplary.

Wellcome Trust ist eine der größten karitativen Stiftungen der Welt. Sie entstand 1936 gemäß dem Testament von Sir Henry Wellcome und hat die Aufgabe, „Forschung mit dem Ziel der Verbesserung der Gesundheit von Mensch und Tier zu unterstützen und zu fördern". Die neue von Hopkins Architects entworfene Zentrale von Wellcome Trust soll alle 600 Mitarbeiter an einem Standort in London unterbringen. Das neue Gebäude mit 28 000 m^2 Nutzfläche liegt neben der ehemaligen Liegenschaft von Wellcome Trust, die Septimus Warwick in den 1930er Jahren im Stil des Greek Revival erbaut hatte und die jetzt renoviert wird. In diesem 16 700 m^2 großen Bau, der gegenwärtig von Hopkins umgestaltet wird, um mehr Tageslicht einfallen zu lassen, sollen eine Bibliothek sowie Räumlichkeiten für Ausstellungen, Vortragsveranstaltungen und Konferenzen untergebracht werden. „Die Arbeiten", sagt der Architekt, „werden die Lesbarkeit des vorhandenen Gebäudes wiederherstellen und eine klare Hierarchie von öffentlichen und privaten Räumlichkeiten schaffen." In dem fast vollständig mit Glas verkleideten Neubau sind zwei Trakte, die an der Euston Road 183–215 beziehungsweise am Gower Place stehen, durch ein bogenförmiges Dach und ein Atrium miteinander verbunden. Im Erdgeschoss sind eine Reihe offizieller Sitzungsräume, eine Passage, ein Café für Mitarbeiter, ein Informationszentrum sowie weitere informelle Räumlichkeiten für Versammlungen untergebracht. In beiden Trakten befinden sich auf den oberen Ebenen Büros, der südliche Bauteil verfügt über ein Dachrestaurant. Hier offenbart sich große Sorgfalt im Umgang mit Details, dabei gelten die Kosten dieses Projekts in Höhe von etwa 3000 Pfund pro m^2 als vorbildlich.

Le Wellcome Trust est l'une des plus importantes institutions charitables du monde. Fondée grâce au legs de Sir Henry Wellcome en 1936, sa mission est de « faciliter et promouvoir la recherche pour améliorer la santé humaine et animale ». Son nouveau siège social, conçu par Hopkins Architects, réunit ses six cents collaborateurs sur un site unique au 183–215 Euston Road à Londres. L'immeuble de 28 000 m^2 est situé à côté du siège d'origine de style néoclassique dessiné par Septimus Warwick dans les années 1930, qui sera rénové. La bibliothèque, les espaces d'exposition, les salles de conférences seront situées dans ce bâtiment de 16 700 m^2 dans lequel Hopkins fera pénétrer la lumière naturelle. « Ce travail », expliquent les architectes, « rétablira la lisibilité du bâtiment existant et créera une hiérarchie claire entre les espaces privés et ceux ouverts au public. » Le nouvel immeuble, presque entièrement habillé de verre, se compose de deux blocs, donnant respectivement sur Euston Road et Gower Place au sud, réunis par un toit incurvé et un atrium. Une série de salles de réunion, une rue intérieure, un café pour le personnel, un centre d'information et des pièces de réunion moins formelles sont répartis au rez-de-chaussée. Les deux blocs sont occupés par des bureaux aux niveaux supérieurs, et un restaurant en toiture au sud. Malgré l'attention soignée aux détails de réalisation, le coût de ce projet, environ 4600 euros le m^2 est considéré comme exemplaire.

The high, wide glass volume of the new building faces Euston Road, while a curving roof creates a large atrium and also covers the smaller structure to the south on Gower Place.

Der hohe, weiträumige Glastrakt des neuen Gebäudes liegt an der Euston Road, während sich über einem geräumigen Atrium ein gebogenes Dach erhebt, das auch den im Süden am Gower Place gelegenen, kleineren Bau einbezieht.

L'important volume de verre du nouveau bâtiment donne sur Euston Road. Le toit incurvé crée un vaste atrium et recouvre une petite construction au sud, sur Gower Place.

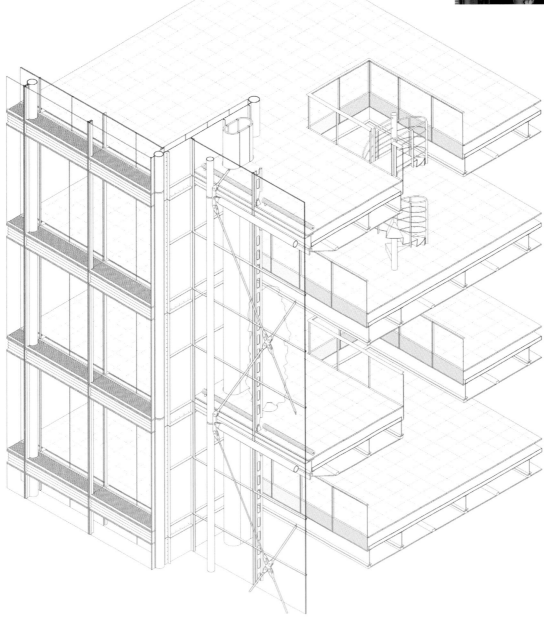

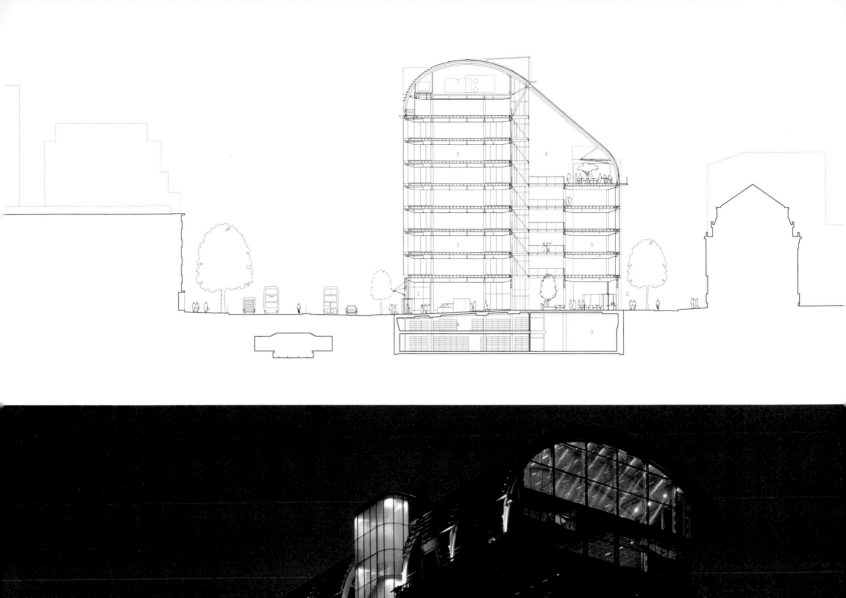

The atrium space is generated by the curving roof linking the two buildings. Although the architecture is manifestly efficient, the atrium allows for breathing space, where some of the 600 staff members can mingle.

Das Atrium entsteht durch die gebogene Dachform, die beide Bauten miteinander verbindet. In der Architektur dieses Gebäudes hält man sich gern auf, zusätzlich bietet das Atrium Raum zum Atmen und für Begegnungen.

Le volume de l'atrium naît de la courbe du toit reliant les deux bâtiments. Quelle que soit par ailleurs l'efficacité du bâtiment, cet atrium offre un espace de respiration où les 600 membres du personnel peuvent se retrouver.

CATHEDRAL REFECTORY NORWICH 2004

FLOOR AREA: 987 m²
CLIENT: The Dean and Chapter of
Norwich Cathedral
COST: £3.2 million

The Refectory of Norwich Cathedral is the first stage of a three-stage project. It occupies the site of the original refectory used by Benedictine monks, and is in scale with the original buildings. This single-story timber structure is set between boundary walls that date to the year 1125. Nine pairs of oak columns support a cast lead panel roof that sits above the basic box-like volume. Triple height spaces contribute to the airy, light atmosphere of the interior. The dining hall is located on the first floor and has an English oak paneled ceiling. Kitchens, offices, and public facilities are set in an oak clad "box" beneath the dining hall. The architects insist on the fact that the primary material, English oak, is used in an "unmistakably modern" way for this building, whose construction cost was £3242 per square meter. The architects write that: "The new building adjoins an ancient English cathedral and as such oak seemed entirely appropriate to use—oak has traditionally been used in ecclesiastical settings as well as having a particularly 'English' character." The building, designed in collaboration with the engineers Buro Happold, was awarded the Gold Medal at the 2004 Wood Awards, intended to "celebrate the standard of joinery and design in timber," at a ceremony held in Carpenters Hall in London. The judges for this award commented that the refectory is "an extremely high quality design that is very intelligently situated and organized and incorporates only the best quality finishes." They further stated that "The workmanship was fantastic throughout, a real achievement in itself." The Hostry building, which will house a new visitors' center, including education suites, a shop, exhibition spaces, and a community room, will constitute phase two of the Cathedral project.

Das Refektorium der Kathedrale von Norwich ist der erste Bau eines Projekts mit drei Bauabschnitten. Es befindet sich am Standort des ehemaligen, von den Mönchen des Benediktinerordens genutzten Refektoriums und entspricht den Proportionen der ursprünglichen Bauten. Der eingeschossige Holzbau wurde zwischen die Begrenzungsmauern aus dem Jahr 1125 eingefügt. 18 Stützen aus Eichenholz tragen ein Tafeldach aus gegossenem Blei, das den einfachen, kastenförmigen Baukörper überdeckt. Die stellenweise dreifache Raumhöhe trägt zur luftigen, hellen Atmosphäre des Innenraums bei. Der Speisesaal befindet sich im ersten Geschoss und ist mit einer Decke aus englischen Eichenpaneelen ausgestattet. Die Küche, Büroräume und öffentliche Einrichtungen sind in einem mit Eichenholz verkleideten „Kasten" unterhalb des Speisesaals untergebracht. Die Architekten betonen die Tatsache, dass das primäre Material, englisches Eichenholz, bei diesem Gebäude mit einem Quadratmeterpreis von 3242 Pfund in „unverkennbar moderner Weise" verwendet wurde. Die Architekten schreiben, „das neue Gebäude grenzt an eine sehr alte englische Kathedrale und deshalb erscheint Eichenholz als sehr passend – Eichenholz wird traditionellerweise bei sakralen Bauten verwendet und

hat darüber hinaus einen spezifisch ‚englischen' Charakter". Das in Zusammenarbeit mit dem Ingenieurbüro Buro Happold entworfene Gebäude wurde anlässlich der Wood Awards 2004 bei einer Feier in der Carpenters Hall in London mit der Goldmedaille ausgezeichnet. Diese wird vergeben, um „ein hohes Niveau im handwerklichen Umgang und in der Gestaltung mit dem Werkstoff Holz auszuzeichnen". Die Preisrichter bemerkten in diesem Fall, dass es sich beim Refektorium um „einen äußerst qualitätvollen Entwurf handelt, der sehr durchdacht platziert und gegliedert ist und bei dem nur bestmögliche Oberflächengestaltungen Verwendung fanden". Darüber hinaus sprachen sie von „durchgängig großartiger Handwerkskunst, an sich betrachtet schon eine wahre Leistung". In der zweiten Phase des Kathedralenprojekts soll ein Gästehaus entstehen mit einem neuen Besucherzentrum und Unterrichtsräumen, einem Laden, Ausstellungsflächen sowie einem Gemeinschaftsraum.

Le réfectoire de la cathédrale de Norwich est la première phase d'un projet qui en compte trois. Il occupe le site du réfectoire originel utilisé par les moines bénédictins, et reste à l'échelle des bâtiments anciens. Cette structure en bois à un étage est insérée entre des murs de clôture qui datent de 1125. Neuf paires de colonnes de chêne soutiennent une toiture en plomb qui recouvre l'ensemble en forme de boîte. Ces espaces triple hauteur contribuent à donner une atmosphère aérée et lumineuse. La salle à manger au premier niveau possède un plafond en panneaux de chêne anglais. Les cuisines, les bureaux et les installations publiques sont situés dans une « boîte » habillée de chêne sous la salle à manger. Les architectes insistent sur le fait que ce matériau de base, le chêne anglais, est utilisé de façon « absolument moderne » dans un projet dont les coûts de construction se sont élevés à 3242 livres le m². Ils expliquent, par ailleurs, que le nouveau bâtiment est adjacent à une très ancienne cathédrale anglaise et que le chêne semblait donc le matériau approprié, puisqu'il a traditionnellement été utilisé dans les bâtiments religieux et qu'il possède un caractère particulièrement « anglais ». Le réfectoire, conçu en collaboration avec les ingénieurs Buro Happold, a reçu la médaille d'or des Wood Awards 2004 (Prix du bois) qui célèbrent la pratique de la menuiserie et de la conception en bois, à l'occasion d'une cérémonie tenue au Carpenter's Hall de Londres. Le commentaire des juges insistait sur le fait que ce réfectoire était « un projet d'une très haute qualité, très intelligemment implanté et organisé et qui fait appel à une finition d'un soin remarquable... Le travail manuel a été fantastique, une vraie réussite en soi ». Le bâtiment de l'aubret, qui abritera un nouveau centre d'accueil pour les visiteurs, dont des installations éducatives, une boutique, des espaces d'exposition et une salle de réunion, constituera la phase 2 du projet.

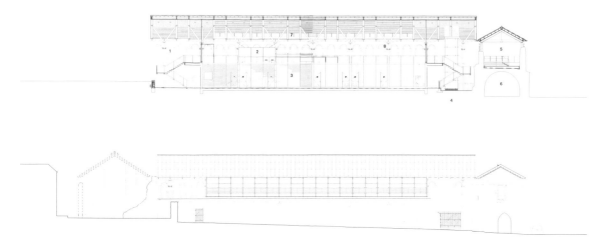

Although it seems quite large in relation to the Cathedral, as seen in the plan to the right, the refectory fits in to the existing site, as the 12th-century boundary walls make visible to the left.

Obgleich es im Grundriss rechts im Verhältnis zur Kathedrale recht groß erscheint, fügt sich das Refektorium in das vorhandene Szenarium ein, so links in die Umfassungsmauern aus dem 12. Jahrhundert.

Assez vaste par rapport à la cathédrale – plan à droite –, le réfectoire est bien adapté à son cadres comme on le voit, par la présence des murs du XIIe siècle à gauche.

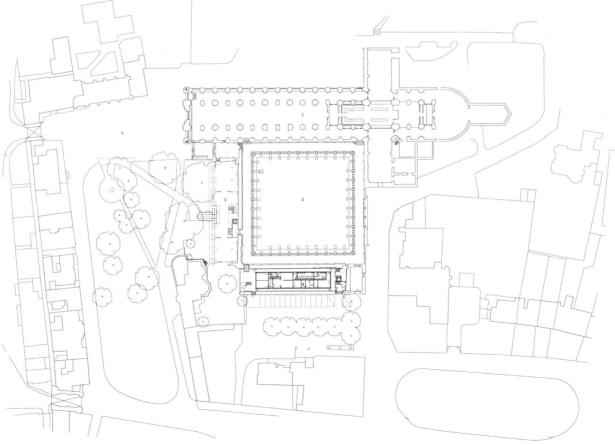

The triple-height ceiling and the use of English oak aid the transition from the old stone environment to a more modern, light-filled space.

Die dreifache Raumhöhe und die Verwendung von altem englischem Eichenholz unterstützen den Übergang von dem alten, steinernen Ambiente zu einem moderneren, lichterfüllten Raum.

Le plafond triple hauteur et le recours au chêne anglais facilitent la transition entre l'ancien bâtiment en pierre et le volume moderne baigné de lumière.

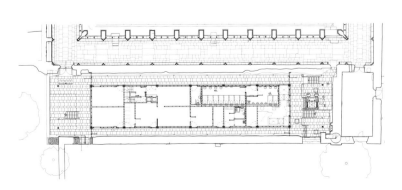

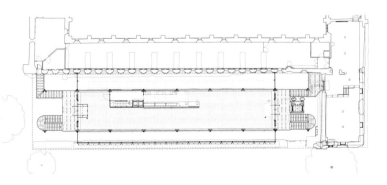

14

EVA JIRICNA

EVA JIRICNA ARCHITECTS
Third Floor
38 Warren Street
London W1T 6AE

Tel: +44 20 75 54 24 00
Fax: +44 20 73 88 80 22
e-mail: mail@ejal.com
Web: www.ejal.com

EVA JIRICNA was born in 1939 in Zlin, Czech Republic. She received a degree in architecture and engineering from the University of Prague (1962), and a postgraduate degree from the Prague Academy of Fine Arts (1963). Jiricna's experience includes working at the Greater London Council on her arrival in the UK in 1968, followed by the Louis de Soissons Partnership and the Richard Rogers Partnership—where she was responsible for the interior design of Lloyd's Headquarters. She became an architect in England in 1973 (Dip. Arch. Royal Institute of British Architects). In 2003, she was elected President of the Architectural Association (AA) in London. Her London office currently employs ten architects and designers, with a satellite office in Prague. Their clients include corporate and public organizations, such as Amec PLC, the Jubilee Line Extension, Andersen Consulting, Boodle & Dunthorne jewelers (featured here), the Royal Academy of Arts, Selfridges, and the Victoria & Albert Museum. With Future Systems, Eva Jiricna designed the Way-In store at Harrods. She is noted for her use of glass and spectacular staircases in the context of integrated design strategies, such as those employed in her interiors for Hugo Boss, Joseph or Joan & David in New York, London, and Paris. More recently, Eva Jiricna worked on the 110-room Hotel Josef in Prague (2002), and a glass and steel structure for the Orangerie in the grounds of Prague Castle. In the UK, Eva Jiricna Architects (EJA) has worked on proposals for the London Docklands Development Corporation and was responsible for the transport interchange at Canada Water on the Jubilee Line. In 1999, EJA designed the Faith Zone as part of the controversial Millennium Dome exhibition.

PRIVATE RESIDENCE BELGRAVIA LONDON 2003

FLOOR AREA: 550 m²
CLIENT: Private Client
COST: not disclosed

This Georgian mid-18th-century house was in extremely bad condition when Eva Jiricna was asked to renovate it. As she points out, in any case, in 1743, Belgravia was something of a suburb of London and not a place for the homes of the wealthy. As she writes, "After consultations with the Planning Officers it was agreed that the front of the house would be restored to its original condition on the ground and first floors, while the rest of the building could be developed into a contemporary space. The 1743 interior at the front, restored to a detailed specification by conservation architect Julian Harrap, now opens up into an airy new single story with a translucent glass roof." A glass staircase connecting all three levels of the house was conceived as a "hinge" between the old and new. New areas of the house have limestone tile floors, while the original house has oak or carpeted floors. Demonstrating her continuing interest in light and the willful contrast of past and present seen both here and in many of her other projects, Eva Jiricna concludes: "The spaces throughout the property, including the swimming pool and garden, change constantly with the light and different perspectives. It is amusing to see the reactions of passers-by when they catch a glimpse of the ultramodern interior stretching out behind the house's 18th-century façade." The floor area of the Belgravia house is 550 m² and the front and rear garden measure 140 m².

Dieses Mitte des 18. Jahrhunderts im georgianischen Stil erbaute Haus befand sich in einem äußerst schlechten Zustand, als Eva Jiricna den Auftrag zu seiner Renovierung erhielt. Sie wies darauf hin, dass Belgravia im Jahr 1743 eine Art Vorstadt von London war und kein Ort für die Häuser der Wohlhabenden. Sie berichtet: „Nach Rücksprache mit den Beamten der Planungsbehörde einigte man sich darauf, dass an der Straßenfront das Haus im ursprünglichen Zustand wiederhergestellt werden sollte, während das übrige Gebäude zu modernen Räumlichkeiten umgestaltet werden konnte. Der vordere Bereich von 1743, der vom Restaurator Julian Harrap nach detaillierter Baubeschreibung rekonstruiert wurde, öffnet sich jetzt nach hinten zu einem luftigen, neuen Einzelgeschoss mit lichtdurchlässigem Glasdach." Ein gläserner Treppenaufgang, der alle drei Ebenen des Hauses miteinander verbindet, ist als Klammer zwischen den alten und neuen

Elementen gedacht. In den neuen Bereichen des Hauses sind die Böden mit Kalksteinfliesen belegt, während das ursprüngliche Haus mit Eichenholzparkett oder Teppichboden ausgestattet ist. Die Architektin beweist einmal mehr ihr Gespür für Lichtführung und den bewussten Kontrast von Altem und Zeitgenössischem und erläutert: „In dem gesamten Objekt sind die Räumlichkeiten, darunter Swimmingpool und Garten, unter dem Einfluss von Licht und wechselnden Blickrichtungen beständiger Veränderung unterworfen. Es ist amüsant, die Reaktionen von Passanten zu beobachten, wenn sie einen Blick auf das ultramoderne Interieur erhaschen, das sich hinter der Fassade aus dem 18. Jahrhundert verbirgt." Das Haus in Belgravia hat eine Fläche von 550 m², die vor und hinter dem Haus gelegenen Grünflächen umfassen 140 m².

La maison de style géorgien du milieu du XVIIIe siècle était en très mauvais état lorsque Eva Jiricna fut appelée pour la rénover. Elle fait remarquer que, en 1743, Belgravia était une sorte de banlieue de Londres et non encore un lieu de résidence pour personnes aisées. « Après consultation des services de l'urbanisme, il fut décidé que la façade serait restaurée dans sa condition d'origine au rez-de-chaussée et au premier étage, tandis que le reste pourrait être transformé en un espace contemporain. L'intérieur de la partie en façade, pris en charge par l'architecte spécialisé dans la restauration historique, Julian Harrap, s'ouvre maintenant sur un vaste volume aéré et protégé par un toit de verre translucide. » Un escalier de verre connecte les trois étages et fonctionne comme une « charnière » entre le neuf et l'ancien. Les parties nouvelles de la maison possèdent des sols en pierre calcaire, ceux de la partie ancienne sont en chêne ou moquettés. Illustrant son intérêt permanent pour la lumière et les contrastes voulus entre le présent et le passé, ici comme dans d'autres projets, Eva Jiricna conclut : « Les espaces environnants, dont la piscine et le jardin, changent continuellement avec la lumière et les perspectives différentes. Il est amusant d'observer les réactions des passants lorsqu'ils aperçoivent un instant l'intérieur ultramoderne qui se déploie derrière la façade XVIIIe siècle de la maison. » La surface au sol de cette résidence urbaine est de 550 m² et les deux jardins, devant et derrière, mesurent 140 m².

One of the architect's trademark glass stairways provides a focal point for the transition to the thoroughly modern single-story area of the refurbishment.

Eines der für die Architektin typischen gläsernen Treppenhäuser markiert den Übergang zu dem gänzlich modernen, eingeschossigen Bereich des umgebauten Hauses.

Un de ces escaliers de verre qui sont la marque de l'architecte constitue le point focal de transition vers la zone restaurée résolument moderne.

To the left, an image looking from the steps leading from the conservatory into the living room, and out toward the swimming pool and garden. This page, the bathroom and, below right, the staircase from the original house (1743). All paneling and doors were restored using period methods. The type of paint is also original.

Links der Blick von der vom Gewächshaus zum Wohnzimmer führenden Treppe und hinaus zu Swimmingpool und Garten. Auf dieser Seite das Badezimmer und rechts darunter die Treppe des alten Hauses von 1743. Sämtliche Wandverkleidungen und Türen wurden mit den damals üblichen Verfahren restauriert. Auch die verwendete Farbe entspricht dem Original.

À gauche, vue prise des escaliers conduisant du jardin d'hiver vers le séjour et au dehors vers la piscine et le jardin. Sur cette page, la salle de bains, et ci-dessous à droite, l'escalier de la maison d'origine datant de 1743. Tous les lambris et les portes ont été restaurés selon des méthodes anciennes. Le type de peinture est lui aussi d'époque.

BOODLE & DUNTHORNE LIVERPOOL 2004

FLOOR AREA: 460 m²
CLIENT: Boodle & Dunthorne
COST: not disclosed

Boodle & Dunthorne have maintained their office and retail premises in the same prominent corner location in Liverpool since 1798. The intention of this refurbishment project was to free up the ground floor as much as possible and restore the rhythm of windows on the upper and lower levels. The windows have been opened up to the street, giving a feeling of space and transparency. As Eva Jiricna writes, "When we were asked to re-design the shop on the ground floor, our first step was to reconsider the external appearance and to persuade the client to change the façade into a more structured form which would return the overall expression of the building to its former glory. The structural grid of the original building had to be respected of course, but it did not prevent us from achieving substantial transparency into the new shop by reducing the amount of solid masonry." A spiral staircase forms a link between the old and the new elements of the shop. The structure of a DNA molecule was an initial source of inspiration for the stair, which forms a natural focal point. Lightness and spaciousness were important throughout the design process and the new displays integrate lighting, display space, and cooling in one functional solution. Again according to the architect, "The product sold on the premises—jewelry—is best viewed in a strong, direct light which maximizes the sparkle of the gemstones and accentuates their form. Glass cabinets allow a clear view of the display and with the application of surface treatments—films, etc.—transparency can be changed to translucency for contrast. The combination of these two systems permits the interior of the premises to be perceived as one large space yet allow for the introduction of semi-private areas to ensure a comfortable environment for customers." The basement level of Boodle & Dunthorne measures 140 m², the ground level 170 m² and the first floor 150 m², with a total of 460 m².

Boodle & Dunthorne unterhalten seit 1798 ihre Büro- und Verkaufsräume an derselben markanten Straßenecke in Liverpool. Diesem Renovierungsprojekt lag die Absicht zugrunde, das Erdgeschoss weitgehend freizulegen und den Rhythmus der Fensterfolge in der oberen und unteren Ebene so weit wie möglich wiederherzustellen. Durch die Öffnung der Fenster zur Straße hin entstand eine Atmosphäre von Geräumigkeit und Transparenz. Eva Jiricna kommentiert: „Als wir den Auftrag erhielten, das Ladengeschäft im Erdgeschoss umzugestalten, beschäftigten wir uns als Erstes mit dem äußeren Erscheinungsbild und überzeugten den Auftraggeber davon, die Fassade stärker zu strukturieren, um so dem Gesamteindruck des Gebäudes seinen früheren Glanz zurückzugeben. Obwohl wir natürlich das konstruktive Raster des ursprünglichen Gebäudes beachten mussten, konnten wir durch die Verminderung des Anteils kompakter Wandfläche in dem neuen Ladengeschäft eine wesentlich größere Transparenz erreichen." Eine Wendeltreppe fungiert als Bindeglied zwischen den alten und neuen Bereichen des Geschäfts.

Der konstruktive Aufbau eines DNA-Moleküls diente als Inspirationsquelle für die Form der Treppe, die wie selbstverständlich im Zentrum steht. Für den Entwurfsprozess spielten Helligkeit und Weite eine große Rolle, und die neuen Vitrinen vereinen Beleuchtung, Präsentation und Kühlung in einer funktionalen Lösung. Die Architektin dazu: „Das hier zu kaufende Produkt – Schmuck – betrachtet man am besten in starkem, direktem Licht, das den Glanz der Edelsteine maximiert und ihre Form hervorhebt. Glasvitrinen gestatten eine gute Sicht auf die Auslage; durch die Behandlung der Oberflächen mit Folien und dergleichen lässt sich der Grad der Transparenz regeln. Die Kombination dieser beiden Systeme lässt das Interieur als einen großen Raum erscheinen und erlaubt zugleich das Einfügen halb privater Bereiche, um der Kundschaft eine angenehme Umgebung zu bieten." Die Souterrainebene von Boodle & Dunthorne umfasst 140 m², das Erdgeschoss 170 m² und der erste Stock 150 m², mithin eine Gesamtfläche von 460 m².

Boodle & Dunthorne occupent les mêmes locaux – commerce et bureaux – sur un angle de rue de Liverpool depuis 1798. L'intention de ce projet de rénovation était de libérer autant que possible le rez-de-chaussée et de rétablir le rythme des ouvertures aux niveaux supérieurs et inférieurs. Les fenêtres ont été réouvertes sur la rue pour donner une sentiment d'espace et de transparence. Comme Eva Jiricna l'écrit : « Lorsqu'on nous a demandé de revoir la conception du magasin du rez-de-chaussée, notre premier geste fut de remettre en question l'aspect extérieur et de persuader le client de modifier la façade sous une forme plus structurée qui réinstallerait l'immeuble dans sa gloire ancienne. La trame structurelle d'origine devait être bien entendu respectée, ce qui ne nous a pas empêché d'atteindre à une transparence substantielle dans le nouveau magasin en réduisant la masse de maçonnerie aveugle. » Un escalier en spirale fait lien entre les éléments nouveaux et anciens du magasin. La logique structurelle d'une molécule d'ADN a inspiré l'escalier qui forme un point d'attraction naturel. La légèreté et le sentiment d'espace étaient importants tout au long du processus de création et les nouveaux aménagement, intègrent éclairage, présentation des produits et climatisation dans une solution fonctionnelle unique. Selon l'architecte : « Le produit vendu – les bijoux – doit se voir sous une lumière forte et directe qui fait ressortir au maximum l'éclat des pierres et souligne leur forme. Des vitrines en verre permettent une vision claire de leur présentation tandis que l'application de traitements de surface – films, etc. – joue de la transparence et de la translucidité pour créer des contrastes. La combinaison de ces deux systèmes donne une perception de vaste espace tout en favorisant l'insertion de zones semi-privées pour offrir un environnement confortable aux clients. » Le sous-sol mesure 140 m², le rez-de-chaussée, 170 m², et l'étage 150 m², soit 460 m² au total.

The architect's mastery of light forms, frequently made at least in part with glass, is visible in these images as is a spectacular but relatively narrow double-helix-shaped stairway (below).

Die Meisterschaft der Architektin im Umgang mit Leuchten, die häufig zumindest teilweise aus Glas bestehen, ist auf diesen Bildern zu sehen, ebenso wie eine spektakuläre, relativ schmale Treppe in der Form einer Doppelhelix (unten).

La maîtrise des formes légères par l'architecte, souvent à l'aide de verre, est notable dans ces images comme, par exemple, dans cet escalier en double hélice spectaculaire mais relativement étroit (ci-dessous).

15

RICHARD ROGERS

RICHARD ROGERS PARTNERSHIP
Thames Wharf
Rainville Road
London W6 9HA

Tel: +44 20 73 85 12 35
Fax: +44 20 73 85 84 09
e-mail: enquiries@rrp.co.uk
Web: www.richardrogers.co.uk

RICHARD ROGERS was born in Florence in 1933. He studied at the Architectural Association (AA) in London, and received his Master of Architecture degree from Yale (1954–59). He was the recipient of the 1985 RIBA Gold Medal and the 2000 Praemium Imperiale. He is a Trustee of the Museum of Modern Art in New York. He founded his present firm, Richard Rogers Partnership, in 1977, just after the completion of the Centre Pompidou. "We were young and we wanted to shock them." This is how Renzo Piano described the design of the Centre Georges Pompidou, Paris (1971–77), which he worked on with Richard Rogers. This goal was attained. Piano and Rogers both joined the ranks of the best-known architects in the world, known for a "High-Tech" style that Rogers affirmed with very visible structures, like the Lloyd's of London Headquarters (1978–86). Rogers subsequently refined his visually complex assemblages in buildings like the Channel 4 Television Headquarters, London (1990–94), and the Law Courts in Bordeaux (1992–98). Richard Rogers has also participated in large-scale urban schemes, such as the Lu Jia Zui master plan (Shanghai, 1992–94). Recent and current work includes the Hesperia Hotel and Conference Centre, Barcelona (1999–2006); Madrid Barajas Airport (1997–2005); Maggie's Centre, London (2001–06); and Terminal 5, Heathrow Airport, London (1989–2008). Another high-profile office project is the National Assembly of Wales in Cardiff.

CHISWICK PARK
LONDON
1999 - 2004

FLOOR AREA: 136 000 m²
CLIENT: Chiswick Park Unit Trust
COST: £130 million

This low-rise business development is located on a 13-hectare site that had building clearance for about 136 000 m² of office space and parking for 1700 cars. The first phase of the project, comprising 53 800 m² with three four-story buildings, was completed at the end of 2000. Phase 2 included 85 600 m² made up of four- and six-story buildings. As the architects describe the exterior appearance of the buildings, "The perimeter steelwork on each building comprises tubular steel elements spanning between the main concrete frame and slender columns spaced 6 m and 9 m away from the building along the side and front elevations. This steelwork supports a number of elements including high-level aluminum anodized louvres, walkways and escape stairs." A large landscaped public area, including an open-air performance area and a lake, serves the complex, with a canopied wooden walkway leading to building entrances running along the lake. Parking areas are located on the perimeter with green "fingers" of landscaped area reaching inward toward the lake. Cladding of the buildings and the planting were designed to reduce traffic noise in the office space. The elegant, lightweight canopies over these buildings and their landscaped environment make them both attractive and efficient.

Dieses Gewerbegebiet befindet sich auf einem 13 ha großen Gelände, auf dem 136 000 m² Bürofläche in relativ flacher Bebauung und 1700 Parkplätze entstehen dürfen. Die erste Phase des Projekts mit drei viergeschossigen Bauten auf insgesamt 53 800 m² wurde Ende 2000 fertig gestellt. Die zweite Phase umfasst vier- und sechsstöckige Bauten mit insgesamt 85 600 m² Fläche. Der Architekt beschreibt das äußere Erscheinungsbild der Bauten so: „Das äußere Stahlgerüst an jedem Gebäude besteht aus Stahlrohrelementen, die den Raum zwischen dem Betonrahmen und den schlanken Stützen überspannen, die im Abstand von 6 bzw. 9 m entlang den Seiten des Gebäudes stehen. Dieses Stahlgerüst trägt eine Reihe von Elementen, darunter Belüftungsklappen aus exloxiertem Aluminium, Laufgänge und Feuertreppen." Zu dem Gewerbegebiet gehört eine öffentlich zugängliche großflächige Grünanlage mit Freiluftbühne und einem See; ein überdachter Holzsteg führt zu den Gebäudeeingängen entlang des Gewässers. Parkmöglichkeiten finden sich am Rand der Anlage, durchzogen von begrünten „Fingern", die nach innen zum See zeigen. Die Verkleidung der Gebäude und die Bepflanzung sind darauf angelegt, den Verkehrslärm zu reduzieren. Die eleganten, leichtgewichtigen Gittergerüste über den Gebäuden und die grüne Umgebung lassen die Anlage gleichermaßen reizvoll und funktionell erscheinen.

Ce parc d'affaires composé d'immeubles de faible hauteur occupe un terrain de 13 hectares sur lequel sont prévus 136 000 m² de bureaux et des parkings pour 1700 véhicules. La phase 1 – trois immeubles de quatre niveaux de 53 800 m² – s'est achevée fin 2000. La phase 2 de 85 600 m² se compose d'immeubles de quatre et six niveaux. L'architecte décrit ainsi l'aspect extérieur du projet : « La charpente métallique périmétrique apparente de chaque immeuble se compose d'éléments tubulaires en acier reliant l'ossature principale en béton et de fines colonnes espacées de 6 à 9 m le long des élévations frontales et latérales. Cette construction soutient un certain nombre d'éléments dont des auvents brise-soleil en aluminium anodisé, des coursives et des escaliers de secours. » Une vaste zone publique paysagée inclut une installation pour spectacles en plein air et un lac, ainsi que des allées en bois protégées qui conduisent aux entrées des immeubles répartis le long du lac. Les parkings sont implantés en périmétrie tandis que des « doigts » de zones paysagées vertes sont orientés vers le lac. L'habillage des immeubles et les plantations ont été conçus pour réduire les bruits de la circulation. Les élégants et légers auvents des immeubles comme les jardins rendent cet environnement à la fois séduisant et très efficace.

Despite a façade-mounted staircase that might appear as a distant echo of the Centre Georges Pompidou in Paris (Piano & Rogers, 1977), the technology here has become less stridently apparent. Sun shades and the louvered grid hovering above the structure give it an appearance of efficient lightness.

Die außen an der Fassade angebrachte Treppe erscheint wie ein fernes Echo des Centre Georges Pompidou in Paris (Piano & Rogers, 1977), die Technik ist hier allerdings weniger augenfällig. Markisen und das über dem Gebäude schwebende Schirmgitter verleihen ihm ein Erscheinungsbild funktionaler Leichtigkeit.

Si l'escalier en façade peut sembler un écho lointain de celui du Centre Pompidou à Paris (Piano et Rogers, 1977), la technologie est ici moins fortement apparente. Des brise-soleil et une grille à ailettes suspendus au-dessus du bâtiment créent une impression de légèreté efficace.

Cheerful furniture, light sun screens and the presence of water make for a most pleasant and comfortable atmosphere. As Renzo Piano described the Center Pompidou: "At the time (1977) we were young and we wanted to be 'in the face' of people who were against contemporary architecture." Both Piano and Rogers have moved onward since that date.

Heitere Möbel, sonnige Abschnitte und das Wasser tragen zu einer freundlichen und behaglichen Atmosphäre bei. Wie Renzo Piano über das Pompidou Center sagte, "damals (1977) waren wir jung und wollten die Leute aufrütteln, die wenig für zeitgenössische Architektur übrig hatten." Sowohl Piano als auch Rogers haben sich seither weiter entwickelt.

Un mobilier de style chaleureux, des protections solaires légères et de l'eau créent une atmosphère plaisante et confortable. Renzo Piano explique : « À l'époque (1977) nous étions jeunes et nous voulions provoquer des gens qui n'étaient pas vraiment enthousiastes pour l'architecture contemporaine. » Piano et Rogers ont beaucoup évolué depuis.

MOSSBOURNE COMMUNITY ACADEMY LONDON 2002-04

FLOOR AREA: 8312 m²
CLIENT: Mossbourne Community Academy Ltd.
COST: £19 million

"This project is all about putting pride back into a community. It is about ownership, equality and heart. It is about genuine approaches to sustainability through environmental design and material choices," declare the architects. Built for the Mossbourne Community Academy Ltd., in one of "England's most deprived boroughs," at a cost of £19 million, this 8312 m² structure was designed to accommodate 900 pupils aged 11 to 16. Richard Rogers has chaired the Urban Task Force that has favored "ideas of urban renewal generated at grassroots level," and the Mossbourne Academy would appear to be a full-scale demonstration of his ideas and ideals. The three-story timber-frame building is located on a triangular site circumscribed on two sides by railway tracks, and looking to the north to the green area of Hackney Downs. Relatively closed façades face the busy railway lines, leaving the open sections of the building to the parkland opposite. A landscaped square creates a visual link with this park area and teaching spaces look out in this direction. Each age group in the school is based in a section of the building described as a "terraced house." Each house has ground-level common space, two levels of classrooms, and a top-lit "IT resource space."

„Bei diesem Projekt ging es darum, einer Gemeinde ihr Selbstbewusstsein zurückzugeben. Es ging um Eigentum, Gleichheit und Herz. Es ging um ernsthafte Wege zu Nachhaltigkeit durch umweltgerechte Gestaltung und Auswahl von Materialien", erläutern die Architekten. Dieser 8312 m² große Bau, der für die Mossbourne Community Academy Ltd. in einem der „am stärksten benachteiligten Stadtbezirke Englands" für 19 Millionen Pfund errichtet wurde, soll Platz für 900 Schüler im Alter zwischen 11 und 16 Jahren bieten. Richard Rogers hatte den Vorsitz in der Urban Task Force, die „Vorstellungen von urbaner Erneuerung aus der Froschperspektive" favorisierte – die Mossbourne Academy schien zu diesen Vorstellungen und Idealen bestens zu passen. Der dreistöckige Holzrahmenbau steht auf einem dreieckigen Grundstück, das auf zwei Seiten von Eisenbahnschienen

begrenzt wird und nach Norden auf den Grünzug der Hackney Downs schaut. Den stark befahrenen Gleisen sind relativ geschlossene Fassaden zugewandt, während sich das Gebäude zu den gegenüberliegenden Grünflächen öffnet. Ein begrünter Platz schafft eine optische Verbindung zur Parklandschaft, zu der die Unterrichtsräume ausgerichtet sind. Jeder Altersgruppe ist ein als „Reihenhaus" bezeichneter Abschnitt des Gebäudes zugeordnet. Jedes Haus verfügt über einen Gemeinschaftsraum im Erdgeschoss, zwei Ebenen mit Klassenräumen sowie einen Computer- und IT-Bereich mit Oberlicht.

« L'objectif de ce projet est de redonner un peu de fierté à la cité. Il parle de propriété, d'égalité et de cœur. Il représente une approche authentique de développement durable à travers une conception environnementale et un choix de matériaux », expliquent les architectes. Construit pour la Mossbourne Community Academy Ltd. dans l'une des « communes les plus défavorisées d'Angleterre » pour un coût de 19 millions de livres, ce bâtiment de 8312 m² peut recevoir 900 élèves âgés de onze à seize ans. R. Rogers a présidé le groupe de travail partisan « d'idées de rénovation urbaine au ras des marguerites » dont la Mossbourne Academy devait être une démonstration à pleine échelle. Le bâtiment à ossature en bois de trois niveaux de haut se dresse sur un terrain triangulaire limité sur deux côtés par des voies de chemin de fer et au nord sur la zone des verte des Hackney Downs. Les façades relativement fermées font face aux voies ferrées, la plus ouverte donnant sur le parc. Un square paysager crée un lien visuel entre ce parc et les salles d'enseignement orientées dans la même direction. Chaque groupe d'âge s'est vu attribuer une section du bâtiment décrit comme un « alignement de maisons ». Chaque « maison » dispose d'un espace commun au rez-de-chaussée, de deux niveaux de salles de cours et d'un « espace de ressources d'information » à éclairage zénithal.

Shaped like a "V" with its closed rear facing railway tracks, this three-story timber-frame building is one of the largest structures of its kind in the UK. It shares its sharp articulation with other work by Rogers, but the use of wood softens its aspect somewhat.

Der v-förmige, dreigeschossige Holzrahmenbau, der seine geschlossene Rückseite den Eisenbahnschienen zuwendet, ist eines der größten Gebäude seiner Art in Großbritannien. Er gleicht mit seiner präzisen Artikulation anderen Bauten von Rogers; der Gebrauch von Holz trägt zur Milderung der Form bei.

En forme de V, dont la pointe fermée donne sur des voies ferrées, cette construction en bois de trois niveaux est l'une de plus grandes réalisations de ce type au Royaume-Uni. Elle reprend le type d'articulation nerveuse d'autres œuvres de Rogers mais à l'aspect quelque peu adouci par le recours au bois.

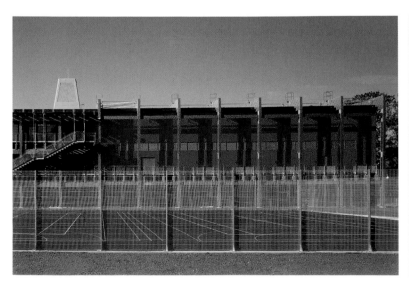

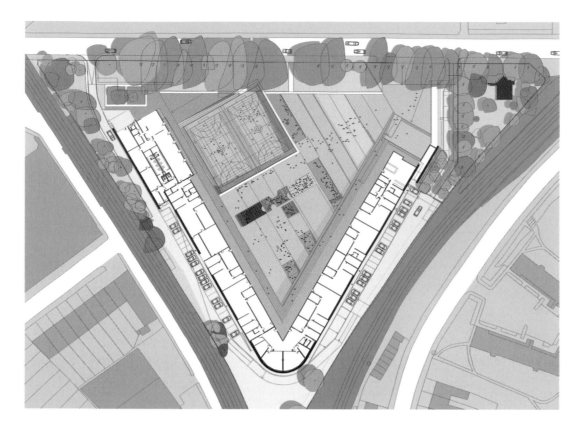

The triangular site of the Academy is circumscribed on two sides by railroad tracks that generate frequent noise, while to the north it looks out onto Hackney Downs, one of the few green spaces in the area.

Das dreieckige Grundstück wird auf zwei Seiten von Eisenbahnschienen begrenzt, was kontinuierlich für Lärm sorgt. Im Norden grenzen die Hackney Downs an das Grundstück, eine der raren Grünflächen der Gegend.

Le terrain triangulaire de l'Académie est bloqué sur deux côtés par des voies ferrées à la circulation bruyante mais donne au nord sur les Hackney Downs, un des rares espaces verts de cette zone.

The recreational zone in the center of the school's "V" form is intended to be the heart of the institution, where students are shielded from the more industrial environment and turned toward the green of Hackney Downs.

Der Pausenbereich im Zentrum des v-förmigen Schulgebäudes ist als Herzstück der Institution gedacht, in dem die Schüler vom industriellen Umfeld abgeschirmt und dem Grünzug der Hackney Downs zugewandt sind.

La zone de récréation au centre du « V » de l'école est le cœur de l'institution. Les étudiants sont protégés de l'environnement industriel et bénéficient d'une vue sur les Hackney Downs.

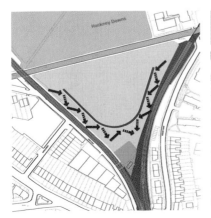

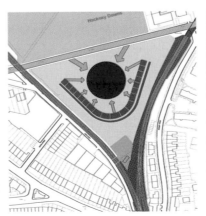

PHOTO CREDITS IMPRINT

CREDITS: PHOTOS / PLANS / DRAWINGS / CAD DOCUMENTS

18, 21–22 top, 23 bottom, 24 top left, 25 top and bottom right, 27–29 top © Timothy Soar/22 bottom, 23 top and center, 29 bottom © Adjaye/Associates / 24 top right and bottom, 25 bottom left © Morley von Sternberg/Arcaid/30–34, 37, 38 top right and bottom © Roderick Coyne of Alsop & Partners/35 © Morley von Sternberg/Arcaid/38 top left, 40–41 © Alain Lai of Alsop & Partners/39 © Alsop Architects/42, 47 © Peter MacKinven/VIEW/45, 46 top, 49–50 top, 51 © Hélène Binet/46 bottom, 50 bottom © Caruso St John Architects/52–56, 58 top, 59 © Edmund Sumner/VIEW/57 bottom, 58 bottom © Chetwood Associates/60–67 © Richard Bryant/Arcaid/64 bottom, 65 top © David Chipperfield Architects/69 © Studio Toni Yli-Suvanto/70–71 © David Chipperfield Architects/72–77 © Dennis Gilbert/VIEW/78–82 top, 87 © Sally Ann Norman/VIEW/82 bottom left and right, 83–86 © Edmund Sumner/VIEW/88–95 © FOA/97–99 © Masterplanning Team: EDAW, FOA, Allies & Morrison, HOK Sport, Buro Happold/100–104, 106 © Grant Smith/VIEW/105 top left and bottom, 116 bottom © Peter Cook/VIEW/105 top right © Dennis Gilbert/VIEW/109–110 top, 111–112 top, 113–116 top, 117 © Raf Makda/VIEW/110 bottom, 112 bottom © Foster and Partners/118–122, 123 bottom, 124–125 top © Edmund Sumner/VIEW/123 top, 125 bottom, 128 bottom, 131 bottom © Grimshaw Architects/127, 128 top left and right, 129 top, 130–131 top © Peter Cook/VIEW/129 bottom left and right/© Chris Gascoigne/VIEW/132–143 © Zaha Hadid Architects/144–148 top, 149 bottom, 150–151 © Nicholas Kane/Arcaid/148 bottom, 149 top, 154 top, 155 bottom, 157 bottom © Hopkins Architects/153, 157 top © Richard Davies/154 bottom, 155 top © Paul Tyagi/156 © Peter MacKinven/VIEW/158–171 © Richard Bryant/Arcaid / 172–175, 178–179 © Grant Smith/VIEW/176–177 © John Maclean/VIEW/181–183, 184 bottom right © Grant Smith/VIEW/184 top, 185 bottom © Richard Rogers Partnership/184 bottom left, 185 © Dennis Gilbert/VIEW

To stay informed about upcoming TASCHEN titles, please request our magazine at www.taschen.com/magazine or write to TASCHEN, Hohenzollernring 53, D-50672 Cologne, Germany, contact@taschen.com, Fax: +49-221-254919. We will be happy to send you a free copy of our magazine which is filled with information about all of our books.

© 2006 TASCHEN GmbH
Hohenzollernring 53, D-50672 Köln
www.taschen.com

PROJECT MANAGEMENT: Florian Kobler, Cologne
COLLABORATION: Barbara Huttrop, Cologne
PRODUCTION: Thomas Grell, Cologne
DESIGN: Sense/Net, Andy Disl and Birgit Reber, Cologne
GERMAN TRANSLATION: Christiane Court, Frankfurt
FRENCH TRANSLATION: Jacques Bosser, Paris

Printed in Italy
ISBN 3-8228-3972-8